WHERE

Lives and Thoughts of

WAS

Holocaust and World War II Survivors

GOD?

With Contributions by

Clara Asscher-Pinkhof

Eva Bross

Tom Fahidy

John and Mania Kay

Rose Kay

Rota Herzberg Lister

David and Genia Lupa

Theodore Milo

Jerzy Tadeusz Pindera

Jan Presser

Jack and Miriam Somer

WHERE

Lives and Thoughts of

WAS

Holocaust and World War II Survivors

GOD?

EDITED BY REMKES KOOISTRA

mosaic press

Canadian Cataloguing in Publication Data

Where was God? : lives and thoughts of Holocaust and World War II survivors

Includes bibliographical references.
ISBN 0-88962-757-6

1. World War, 1939-1945 – Religious aspects. 2. Holocaust, Jewish (1939-1945) – Personal narratives. 3. World War, 1939-1945 – Personal narratives. 4. Holocaust survivors – Canada – Biography. I. Kooistra, Remkes, 1917- .

D804.195W43 2001   940.53'18'0922   C2001-930342-4

Published by Mosaic Press, offices and warehouse at 1252 Speers Road, Units 1 and 2, Oakville, Ontario, L6L 5N9, Canada and Mosaic Press, PMB 145, 4500 Witmer Industrial Estates, Niagara Falls, NY, 14305-1386, U.S.A.

Mosaic Press acknowledges the assistance of the Canada Council and the Department of Canadian Heritage, Government of Canada for their support of our publishing programme.

ISBN 0-88962-757-6
Printed and Bound in Canada.

MOSAIC PRESS, in Canada:
1252 Speers Road, Units 1 & 2,
Oakville, Ontario
L6L 5N9
Phone/Fax: 905-825-2130
mosaicpress@on.aibn.com

MOSAIC PRESS, in U.S.A.:
4500 Witmer Industrial Estates
PMB 145, Niagara Falls, NY
14305-1386
Phone/Fax: 1-800-387-8992
mosaicpress@on.aibn.com

Le Conseil des Arts   The Canada Council
du Canada   for the Arts

This book is dedicated

to the nation of Israel

in memory of the six million Jews

who died in the Holocaust

The publishers have given permission to use excerpts from the following copyrighted works:

From *And Peace Never Came* by Elisabeth M. Raab. Copyright 1997 by Wilfrid Laurier University Press.

From *Danseres Zonder Benen* by Clara Asscher-Pinkhof, 17th edition. Copyright 1984 by Leopold U.M.

From *The Destruction of the Dutch Jews* by Jacob Presser, trans. by Arnold Pomerans. Copyright 1969 by E. P. Dutton & Co., Inc.

From *From the Kingdom of Memory* by Elie Wiesel. Copyright 1990 by Summit Books, a division of Simon & Schuster. Publication rights owned by Georges Borchardt, Inc., New York, NY.

From *Hel en Hemel van Dachau* (*Hell and Heaven of Dachau*) by J. Overduin, trans. by Harry der Nederlanden. Copyright by Paideia Press.

From *Historical Atlas of the Holocaust / United States Holocaust Museum*. Copyright 1996 by Simon & Schuster Macmillan.

From *The Jewish Thought of Emil Fackenheim* by Emil L. Fackenheim. Copyright 1987 by Wayne State University Press.

From *Letters and Papers from Prison* by Dietrich Bonhoeffer. Copyright 1953 by The Macmillan Company.

From *De Nacht der Girondijnen* by Jacques Presser. Copyright 1957 by J. M. Meulenhoff Publishing Company.

From *Nazihel* by Willem van de Pol. Copyright by Van Holkema & Warendorf, renewed by Unieboek Publishing.

From *The Night of the Girondists* by Jacques Press, trans. by Barrows Mussey. Copyright 1992 by The Harvill Press.

From *Post-Holocaust Dialogues: Critical Studies in Modern Jewish Thought* by Steven T. Katz. Copyright 1983 by New York University Press.

From *Star Children* by Clara Asscher-Pinkhof. Copyright 1986 by Wayne State University Press.

From *Wie heeft daar woorden voor?* (*Deliver Us from Evil: Is Something Wrong Between God and Me?*) by William R. Van der Zee, trans. by Gerard M. Verschuuren. Copyright Genesis Publishing Company, 1996.

Permission to use a copy of the painting "Self Portrait with Jewish Identification Card," 1943, in the collection of the Nedersaksische Saving Bank Institute has been given by the owner of the collection, Felix Nussbaum Haus Osnabrück.

TABLE OF CONTENTS

PART III: BEYOND SURVIVAL

ACKNOWLEDGMENTS

Having almost finished my work on this book, I am reminded of this commonplace: "This book would never have been written without the help of..." I feel indebted to many friends who assisted me in one way or another. If I have overlooked some dear helpers, accept my apologies, please.

I thank Judy Wubnig for initiating this study and assisting me in many ways. I also thank her for reading, correcting, and assisting in editing the manuscript.

I thank Marilyn Regehr for her valuable help in doing this project and letting me quote from her thoughtful essay.

I thank Marsha Blok for her bibliographical research and other valuable advice, and Barbara Pressman for her informative contributions to get us started.

I thank the *Social Sciences and Humanities Grant Committee* of the University of Waterloo for its financial help, and especially Joan Hadley for her help and encouragement.

I thank the *Committee on Jewish Studies* at the University of Waterloo and its chairman, Dr. Paul Socken, for their generous financial help towards the publication of this book.

I thank Arlene Sleno, our expert academic secretary at St. Paul's college; Dr. Peter Frick, my successor at St. Paul's college; and the Rev. J.C. Derksen. All three were always willing to assist me in any computer problem I encountered. I also thank my grandson Casey VandePutte, student at the University of Waterloo, for solving many of my technical problems. I thank the technicians of the office of Distance Education at the University of Waterloo for their help in recording the interviews.

I thank Adrian Peetoom for his skilled help in editing several chapters of this book. I owe my deep gratitude to Judy Tanis Parr and William Johnstone Parr for their efforts in editing the entire book and preparing it for publication.

I thank those who wrote their own valuable contributions to this book. A special heartfelt "Thank you" to Rota Herzberg Lister and Jerzy Tadeusz Pindera. Their participation and friendship have been a tremendous encouragement to me. Both provided me with photographs, maps, and chronologies. I also thank Tom Fahidy for his story.

I thank The Harvill Press, London, for allowing me to quote from the work of Jacob Presser.

To Fieke Langer-Asscher, the youngest daughter of Clara Asscher-Pinkhof, I owe my warm thanks for allowing me to translate and quote several parts of her mother's moving autobiography, *Danseres Zonder Benen* [*Ballerina Without Legs*].

And, in a very special way, my warm, heartfelt thanks for the survivors we interviewed, who welcomed us into their homes and shared their often painful memories. What they did will remain an important record of a sad history. May it help future generations to say "Never again!"

Finally, I thank Janette, my wife, for her interest in this project and for helping me to find the time for finishing this book.

Rem Kooistra,
Brampton, Ontario
September 2000

I owe the dead my memory....

To remember is to create links between past and present, between past and future....

The aim of memory is to restore its dignity to justice.

—— Elie Wiesel
From the *Kingdom of Memory*

part one
HISTORY

chapter one
INTRODUCTION

I. Historical Note

The Holocaust was the culmination of centuries of persecution of the Jews. Throughout their history they were persecuted repeatedly in most area of what had been the Roman Empire. But the persecution greatly intensified in the 1930s, especially in Germany.

The word "Holocaust" derives from the Hebrew word *olah* and from a Greek word meaning "burnt offering." It refers to early Jewish worship rituals (see Exodus 25-28, 35-39). The "Holocaust" means the "systematic, state-sponsored murder of six million Jews and millions of non-Jews by the Nazis and their collaborators during World War II." [1]

II. Background of This Book

This book has deep roots in my personal history. I was born and raised in a rather strict Calvinistic family. In our home and church we were instructed to have great respect for the Jewish people. Had not the apostle Paul written "Did God reject his people? By no means!" (Romans 11:1, NIV), and had Paul not called the Jewish people "loved on account of the patriarchs" (Romans 11:28, NIV)? We were not allowed to forget that the Jews were the people of God's covenant. Though in our tolerant Dutch country there was not much open anti-Semitism, I became steadily more aware of the persecution of Jews in Germany and other parts of Europe.

A Jewish girl named Carla Nathans made a deep and lasting impression on me in my middle to late teen years. I knew she was a Jew because she would miss class on Jewish holidays such as *Jom Kippur.* Though I was not in love with her, I liked Carla very much. I can still imagine her sitting at her desk in the next row diagonally in front of me. I liked her fresh enthusiasm and the way she diligently struggled with the difficulties of learning Latin.

In 1935 or 1936 our history class discussed Adolf Hitler and his National Socialism. Our history teacher, Jacob Colpa,[2] himself a Jew, tried to deny the gathering storm of persecution by making light of "the yelling painter of Germany." (Perhaps his ridicule was an effort to quench his own fears or to dispel ours.) But Carla could not stomach any jokes on this matter. Her dark brown eyes with their large dark pupils opened wide in panic and anguish. Her response resembled that of a helpless little lamb in the claws and jaws of a fierce lion. She reminded me of a beautiful wild animal hopelessly trapped. This picture of Carla etched itself in my brain, inspiring me to the courage and compassion that I would need later.

After summer vacation Carla did not return to our school. Rumors spread that the entire Nathans family had escaped to the United States. If Carla is still alive, she would be in her eighties.[3]

During World War II I lived in the Netherlands, first as a student, later as a young minister in my first congregation. I became ever more aware of the persecution of the Jews in my own country, and I tried to help as many of them as I could. More about this part of my life is in the chapter "My War Years."

In 1973 I accepted an appointment as a chaplain at the University of Waterloo and at Wilfrid Laurier University, also in Waterloo. Marsha Blok, librarian at the Dana Porter library at the University of Waterloo, like me an immigrant from the Netherlands, introduced me to The Committee on Jewish Studies and the Holocaust.

During the winter semester of 1985/86, the Chairman of the Committee, Dr. Judy Wubnig of the Philosophy Department,

4

recommended that the oral histories of a number of survivors of the Holocaust and World War II living in the Waterloo-Kitchener area be recorded. These survivors were getting on in age, and the stories of their experiences should not be lost. And it came to pass that the lot fell on me.

In preparation for my new task, I wrote to Dr. Terry Anderson, Assistant Director to the Fred Roberts Crawford Witness to the Holocaust Project at the Emory University in Atlanta, Georgia. From him I received a helpful videocassette titled *Religious Implications of the Holocaust.* The Lacolle Centre of the Concordia University in Montreal provided additional helpful information about doing an oral history project. The Canadian Jewish Congress in Montreal and its Director, Jane Bendow, encouraged our project.

Joan Hadley, Director of the University of Waterloo's Social Sciences and Humanities Grant Fund, gave us valuable advice resulting in a donation of $1000.00 from this fund. Most of the work was done *pro deo*. Barbara Pressmann provided me with a good list of names and addresses of survivors of the Holocaust in the Kitchener-Waterloo area.

We announced our project in *The Gazette*, the university paper, with this message:

Professor Rem Kooistra ... will be interviewing survivors of the destruction of the Jews by the Nazis. The archives will be used for scholarly research and will eventually be deposited with the Canadian Jewish Congress. Any information about survivors will be appreciated.

Next we composed a "Letter of Informed Consent" to be signed by those who would be interviewed, in which we stated that all the collected information would be "used for the purpose of research or instruction."

A gifted student in the Department of Religious Studies, Marilyn Regehr, assisted in the administration of the project. We asked all survivors to tell us about their life and their faith during the time of their incarceration in concentration camps. For this part of our project we were guided the list of different religious responses to the Holocaust mentioned by Steven T. Katz in his *Post-Holocaust Dialogues.* [4]

III. The Interviews

Marilyn Regehr and I began interviewing the survivors in October 1986. On those often cold and snowy nights, we were warmly received by all of the survivors we visited. Nobody objected to our doing this work though not being Jewish ourselves. The resulting nine tapes were preserved, and the stories were transcribed and edited for readability. Several of the survivors have died since then, but their stories are not forgotten.

Drawing from the interviews, Marilyn Regehr wrote an essay titled "Oral History and Theology of the Holocaust." She wondered how the Jewish people in the concentration camp felt about being God's chosen people. Would this belief still be their strength and comfort, or would they wish, like Tevye in *The Fiddler on the Roof,* to be a little less chosen? She found that about half of the survivors with whom she spoke did in fact hold to such a belief, "some comparing the Jewish people to the suffering servant of Isaiah 53, others feeling the Jewish people were the innocent ones suffering for the sins of the world. The other half of the people interviewed held to no such notion, some responding quite negatively 'Chosen for what?'" According to one survivor, "the concept of 'the chosen people' is a sad joke and one of the blackest comedies ever. Another attributed Jewish suffering not to any type of special status but rather to simple historical misfortune."

She found unanimous support for the establishment of the state of Israel. Most of the survivors had either lived in or visited Israel and believed that the Holocaust had helped establish that nation. Some saw Israel as a father or mother providing protection for her children. Said one, "if such a nation had existed during World War II, there would have been 'someone to holler and holler loudly!'"

Must of the survivors that were interviewed believed in the existence of God though they may have experienced a time of doubt while in concentration camps. One woman said that she had her doubts over whether or not God existed when she was in the camps and smelling burning flesh but after the war her beliefs were strengthened once again.

People often stated that they did not know why such horrible events happened. How could God not know what was happening?

Many experienced nightmares and bad dreams long after their release from the camps. One woman stated that on certain mornings when her husband would get up, he would say to her, "I was in camp tonight." Several survivors would not consent to an interview because they feared that the pain awakened by their memories would be too difficult to bear.[5]

Though many of the survivors affirmed that they were not bitter against the German nation, they believed that individuals who had caused harm, no matter how old they were when apprehended, should be brought to justice. After the war, they tended to focus less on their suffering and more on the miracle of survival. Most looked forward to resuming their living and building families.

IV. The Title

One of my dear friends suggested that the title of this book be *Where Was God?* There is no simple answer and yet we need an answer. The question unveils the deepest of all despairs. It shows humanity in its existential lostness. If God is not there, then there is no refuge left. I felt this "hopelessness" every day while writing this book. I asked myself, "if God is the Great I Am, the One who is, and who was, and who is to come, then why was there Auschwitz? Why did God not do anything, or why does it seem that God did not do anything?"

Yet, whoever carefully reads what happened in the death camps will not only see the powers of evil but also see glimpses of God's grace and power, signs of a victory of hope, of survival. Being killed by brutal cruelty may become the way of being lifted up out of misery by the caring, loving hands of God.[6]

Psalm 130 has a double title. It is the song *de profundis*: "Out of the depths I cry to you, O LORD" (NIV), it begins, and yet, at the same time, it is a song *hammaàloth*, a song of the ascent. Going down may become going up.

7

I hope that the title and content of this book may somehow affirm God's presence, even in Auschwitz.

V. The Chapters

The book consists of three parts: "History," "Survivors of the Holocaust," and "Beyond Survival."

In "History," Chapter 1 presents information about how this book was conceived and created. Chapter 2 presents a chronology showing that throughout their history the Jews suffered from persecution and were threatened by extermination. Chapter 3 presents a chronology of the main events before and during World War II. Chapter 4 summarizes the events of the destruction of the Jews in the Netherlands during World War II. In other countries the process was similar. Chapter 5 considers the question, "Where was God during the time of the intended extinction of so many of the Jewish people?"

"Survivors of the Holocaust" contains stories of Holocaust survivors who had lived in Germany, Holland, Hungary, and Poland. The genocide during World War II, also called the "final solution," was intended to kill all the Jews and many others. The Nazis did not succeed; they killed "only" six of the ten million Jews living in Europe at the time of World War II. "*Lass' mich sterben*" ["Let me die"] shows a tiny glimpse of God's grace demanding some compassion from the cruel oppressor, allowing the prisoner to die a "natural" death. Are we allowed to see a ray of God's presence in the dark realm of evil. Does God triumph over Satan? "Death March: the Bitter Choice," the final chapter of this section, is the story of an officer of the Polish army, who, accused of being involved in the Resistance movement, spent five long years in several concentration camps and in the end escaped death only by a perilous flight into the woods. It reveals the painful dilemmas arising from compassion in intense danger.

"Beyond Survival" focuses on stories that reveal conflicts of conscience and obligation and that demonstrate acts of courage and compassion amidst the horrors of the Holocaust. "My War Years" includes the story of my father, who like so many in Holland was arrested because of "underground involvement." Though his imprisonment lasted only four months, he escaped death only narrowly. "The Star" reveals the resolution of inner conflict caused by the oppressor, a conflict between obedience and protest. "The Westerbork Train," the single work of fiction among the other autobiographical stories, tells how the cruelty of the oppressor could become too much even for faithful collaborators. There comes a moment when human conscience cannot tolerate the stress any more and forgets about its own safety and survival.

Libri sua fata habent. Books have their own destinies, but often there is something more that determines their content and shape. To some extent they take on a life of their own, not only recording history but perhaps influencing the future. May the stories in this book be an influence toward courage, compassion, and goodness.

Notes

1. *Historical Atlas of the Holocaust / United States Holocaust Museum* (New York: Simon & Schuster Macmillan, 1996), p. 9. In addition to the extermination of approximately six million Jews, the Nazis also exterminated large numbers of Jehovah's Witnesses, clergy, male homosexuals, Soviet prisoners of war, retarded or emotionally disturbed persons, and especially Roma (Gypsies). Those victims totaled an estimated three-to-five million.

2. Colpa seems to be a transliteration and Latinization of Polac or Polak.

3. If she reads this book, the author would appreciate hearing from her.

4. A complete list of these responses can be found in Chapter 5: In Search of an Answer: Where was God?

5. My father, who was in the concentration camp of Wilhelmshafen as a political prisoner, hardly ever talked about his time in the camp except for the last months of his life.

6. Jesus, when he died on the cross, exclaimed: "'Father, into your hands I commit my spirit'" (Luke 23:46, NIV). These words echo Psalm 31:5 (NIV):

"Into your hands I commit my spirit; redeem me, O LORD, the God of truth." The experience of Jesus and of the Psalm is this: through the depths *de profundis* to the dwelling place and the heart of God.

chapter two

CHRONOLOGY OF
2000 YEARS OF PERSECUTION

38 B.C.E.   Anti-Jewish riots in Alexandria, Egypt; many Jews were killed.

19 C.E.   Emperor Tiberius expels Jews from Rome.

circa 200 C.E. Tertullian, a Church Father, writes his Anti-Jewish polemic, *Adversus Judaeos.*

325 C.E.   Council of Nicaea declares that Jews must continue to exist in seclusion and humiliation.

circa 400   St. John Chrysostom denounces Jews of Antioch.

438   Theodosius II legalizes civil inferiority of the Jews.

circa 630   Policy of forcible conversion of the Jews in the Frankish kingdom.

circa 700   Policy of forcible conversion of the Jews in Spain.

1012   Emperor Henry II of Germany expels Jews from Mains, the beginning of persecution against the Jews in Germany.

1096   First Crusade; thousands of Jews are massacred in
            central Europe.

1215   Fourth Lateran Council introduces the Jewish badge and
            decrees perpetual servitude of Jews.

1290   Expulsion of the Jews from England, first of the great
            general expulsions of the Middle Ages.

1298   In a massacre led by the German knight Rindfleisch,
            thousands of Jews of Central and Southern Germany are
            killed.

circa 1310 Expulsion of the Jews from France.

1480   Inquisition established in Spain by Ferdinand and Isabella
            after centuries of tolerance and peaceful co-existence of
            Christians, Jews, and Muslims.

1492   Expulsion of the Jews from Spain.

1510   Expulsion of the Jews from Brandenburg, Germany.

circa 1650 Decade of pogroms in Poland.

1711   Johann Andreas Eisenmenger writes *Entdecktes
            Judenthum [Judaism Unmasked]*, a denunciation of
            Judaism which had a formative influence on modern
            anti-Semitic polemics.

1819   "Hep! Hep!" riots against Jews in Germany.

1878   Adolf Stöcker, German anti-Semitic preacher and

politician, founds the Christian Social Workers Party, which marks the beginning of the political anti-Semitic movement in Germany.

1879   Influential German historian Heinrich von Treitschke supports anti-Semitic campaigns in Germany.

1879   Wilhelm Marr, German agitator, coins the term "anti-Semitism."

circa 1880   Pogroms in Russia.

1882   First International anti-Jewish congress in Dresden, Germany.

1893   Karl Lueger establishes the Christian Social Party in Vienna, based on anti-Semitic policies.

1894–1906   Dreyfus falsely accused of treason in France.

1899   Houston S. Chamberlain, anti-Semitic author, publishes *Die Grundlagen des 19. Jahrhunderts* [*The Foundations of the Nineteenth Century*], a basis for Adolf Hitler's ideology.

1905   First Russian edition of *The Protocols of the Elders of Zion.*

1920   Adolf Hitler becomes leader of the National Socialist German Workers' Party (NSDAP).

1920   Anti-Semitic articles were published in Henry Ford's newspaper in the United States.

1925   Adolf Hitler's *Mein Kampf* is published.

1933   Hitler becomes Chancellor in Germany; anti-Jewish legislation begins.

1935   Nuremberg laws eliminate citizen rights of Jews.

1938 November 9 & 10
             Kristallnacht, nationwide pogrom against Jewish businesses, synagogues, and homes.

1939 September 1
             Outbreak of war against Poland; beginning of the Holocaust.

1940   Jewish ghettoes created in Poland.

1942 January 20
             Wannsee Conference coordinates plans for the "final solution."

For additional information about the history of anti-Semitism, see the following books:

Katz, Steven T. *The Holocaust in Historical Context. Vol. I: The Holocaust and Mass Death Before the Modern Age.* New York and Oxford: Oxford University Press, 1994.

Paris, Erna. *The End of Days, A Story of Tolerance, Tyranny, and the Expulsion of the Jews from Spain.* Amherst, New York: Prometheus Press, and Toronto: Lester Publishing Ltd., 1995.

Patterson, Charles. *Anti-Semitism: The Road to the Holocaust and Beyond.* New York: Walter and Company, 1982.

Poliakov, Léon. *The History of Anti-Semitism.* Vols. 1-4. Trans. from French by Richard Howard. New York: Vanguard Press, 1965–1985.

Wistrich, Robert S. *Antisemitism: The Longest Hatred.* New York: Pantheon Books, 1991.

chapter three

SHORT CHRONOLOGY
OF WORLD WAR II

1889-1945	Lifetime of Adolf Hitler. Around 1930 he becomes the founder of the NDSAP, the National Democratic Socialistic Arbeiters (Laborers) Party, and proclaims himself to be the *Führer* (leader), not just of the party, but of all of Germany.
1933 January 30	Hitler becomes Reichs Chancellor of Germany.
1938 March	Annexation of Austria by Germany.
1938 September	Annexation of the Sudetenland district of Czechoslovakia. Neville Chamberlain, England's prime minister, meets with Hitler in an attempt to avoid war and agrees to partition Czechoslovakia to preserve "peace." Hitler promises that he has no additional territorial claims.
1939 March	German occupation of Czechoslovakia.
1939 September I	Germany invades Poland.

1939 September 3   England and France declare war on Germany in accordance with a former agreement.

1940 April   Germany invades Denmark and Norway.

1940 May 10   Germany invades the Netherlands, Luxembourg, Belgium, and France (without a declaration of war).

1940 May 14   Germany bombards Rotterdam in the most dramatic example of military *Blitz Krieg* (war as fast as lightning).

1940 May   Capitulation of the Dutch army after courageous defenses with mainly outdated material. Belgium, Luxembourg, and France also capitulate. In the Netherlands Hitler establishes a civil government, headed by a Nazi commissioner, Arthur Seyss-Inquart.

1941 June   Germany invades Russia.

1941 December 7   Japan attacks the U.S. naval base at Pearl Harbor. The U.S. joins the Allied forces in the war against Germany and Japan.

1942   During the early years of the war Hitler seems to be invincible, but by the end of 1942 the tide turns. The Germans are thrown back at Stalingrad. The Allies defeat the German and Italian troops at El Alamein in North Africa.

1943 June   Allied forces invade Italy.

1943 September | Italy surrenders.

1944 June 6 | D Day. Allied forces land in Normandy, France.

1944 fall | Allied paratroops land at Arnhem, the Nether lands, in an attempt to force a quick ending of the war. This endeavor, known as one bridge too far, fails. Many people from the southern parts of the Netherlands are transported to the north by German authorities. In the western provinces many die from hunger and cold in the severe winter of 1944–1945.

1944 December | The Germans counterattack during the Battle of the Bulge in the Ardennes along the eastern border of Belgium, Luxembourg, and France. The Germans fail.

1945 April 30 | Russian [Soviet] forces fight their way into Berlin. Hitler commits suicide.

1945 May 2 | Berlin surrenders.

1945 May 7 | Germany surrenders unconditionally.

chapter four

HISTORY OF THE
PERSECUTION OF THE DUTCH JEWS
DURING WORLD WAR II

The persecution of the Dutch Jews was similar to what happened in other occupied countries. For this chapter I have relied heavily upon Dr. Jacob Presser's *Ondergang: De Vervolging en Verdelging van het Nederlandse Jodendom 1940-1945* (*The Destruction of the Dutch Jews*).[1]

I. Towards Isolation (May 1940–December 1941)

During the first few months of the German occupation, the Dutch Jews were very confused. Many realized that they should have left earlier. Some escaped to Belgium, France, Spain, and Portugal. From there, they went on to England or the United States. A few even managed to escape after the capitulation on May 14, 1940. Some escaped (often for much money) by boat from Scheveningen or IJmuiden to England. Many others believed the German assurances: *"Gegen die Synagoge in Holland haben wir nichts vor"* (We have no plans against the Dutch Synagogue).[2] Knowing what was happening with the Jews in Germany, a number of Jews committed suicide.[3]

In May 1940 it became very clear that our fight was not with just with a hostile nation or state but rather with a hostile ideology with its own particular philosophy and religion: the cult of *Blut und Boden,* a deification of race and country. From this point of view it is understandable that the Nazi occupation began with a cultural attack. The day after the Dutch capitulation, the German head of the news media, Mr. H. Hushahn, fired the Jewish members of the ANP, the Dutch news services. The Nazis had the mistaken notion that the entire Dutch press was dominated by Jews and Communists and, in particular, by Jewish Communists. However, the membership list of Dutch journalists showed that of the 700 Dutch journalists only 37 were Jews. Similarly, among the 400 directors of newspapers only one was a Jew.

Some daring opponents of the Nazi regime started a bi-weekly which they sarcastically called *De Doodsklok, Volksblad bij de opruiming van het Jodendom (The Death Clock, A People's Paper at the Clearance of Jewry)*. It appeared during the summer of 1940 for about five weeks, but then Mr. Hushahn saw it and, of course, *The Death Clock* was forbidden.[4]

Heinrich Heine's poems were not to be sold, but secretly they became widely coveted and cherished. Books by Martin Niemöller, a decorated U-Boat captain from World War I but an opponent of the Nazi philosophy, also were on the list of forbidden literature, and Niemöller himself was sent to prison as were many other intellectuals.

In January 1941, all Dutch Jews [approximately 150,000] were required to be "registered" by the government; the vast majority complied. Soon Dutch Jews were no longer allowed to serve in government positions. Then the Nazi authorities demanded that all educators had to sign either a form A ("I am of the Aryan race") or a form B ("I am a Jew and have Jewish ancestors"). Most people complied with the order, not realizing what was lying ahead.

The isolation of the Jews continued. Soon restaurants and stores were closed to Jews. On January 4, 1941, Jews were forbidden to walk on the *Leidse Plein*, the central plaza of Amsterdam.

In Amsterdam on February 22 and 23, 1941, the first *razzia* (raid in which groups of people were chased, harassed, and arrested) took place.[5] Some 400 Jewish young men of the *Jordaan*, a ghetto-like area of the city where Jews had lived for many generations, were deported, first to a Dutch camp in Schoorl, north of Amsterdam, and then on February 27 to Buchenwald in central Germany, on "a journey without food but with plenty of viciousness." [6] In Buchenwald they met a number of Dutch "political" prisoners who pitied these young men who neither realized nor imagined what was going to happen to them. From Buchenwald they were transported to Mauthausen in north-central Austria because the German SS authorities were not happy with the letters these young Jews had been writing to the Netherlands. Here they were treated more cruelly than before. Mauthausen was a death-camp. When a representative of the Dutch churches asked a German officer why so many of the Dutch Jews died so fast in Mauthausen, the answer was, "Is it our fault that they choose to jump off mountains?" [7] Yet in the official documents diseases such as sunstoke, dysentery, and heart and kidney failure were mentioned as causes of death with typical German meticulousness.

Because of the first raid, a spontaneous general strike took place in Amsterdam on February 25 and 26, 1941. This February strike encouraged the Dutch Jews, showing them that they were not forgotten. It also made the non-Jewish community aware of what kind of rulers Hitler had forced onto the Dutch. Asscher and Cohen of the Jewish Council were told by the SS bosses that Jews had organized the strike and thus were responsible. One of the threatening reprisals the angry officer barked at them was that, if the strike was not over the next day, 500 Jews would be shot to death. The strike ended, but the resistance grew.[8]

In their anti-Semitic activities, the Nazi authorities in the Netherlands employed many Jews themselves. Early in 1941 they established a Jewish Council which was to be held responsible for preserving order in the Jewish quarter of Amsterdam. The Jewish Council had two chairmen: A. Asscher, a diamond dealer; and D. Cohen, a professor. Although the Jewish Council tried to help their people, they were actually instrumental in the destruction of the Dutch Jews.[9]

Soon Professor Leo Polak, a prominent Jew at the University of Groningen, was arrested as "the most dangerous man in Groningen." [10] One of the most widely respected Jews in the nation, Polak had enthusiastically defended the Dutch and had openly refused to give up any of his rights as a citizen.

Isolating measures intensified. Beginning in May 1941, Jewish physicians and dentists were told that they could treat only Jewish patients. One courageous Jewish doctor in Leiden sent each of his patients a letter surrounded by a black mourning border to thank them for the confidence and friendship he had enjoyed from them during many years.

A second raid took place on June 11, 1941. The Jews were accused of trying to destroy an army office by a powerful bomb. The Germans then claimed the "right" to confiscate the possessions of several Jews and to arrest a large number of them for work camps. These too ended up in Mauthausen, and most of them died there.

By the end of this first year, the registration and isolation of the Jews was almost completed.

II. From Isolation to Deportations (September 1941–July 1942)

By autumn 1941 Jews were prohibited from public schools, public parks, technical colleges, public meetings, public libraries, theaters, concerts, sports-grounds, swimming pools, and public markets. Barred from existing symphony orchestras, several dozen Jewish musicians formed their own orchestra and performed 25 concerts from November 1941 to July 1942, when mass deportations began.[11]

During 1942 raids took place in several provinces of the Netherlands. Jews in places such as Arnhem, Enchede, and Oldenzaal were arrested and transported to Mauthausen. One innocent boy who could not find a seat in the train asked the conductor where he had to sit. This conductor hissed, "Get lost," and so the young man survived; only his suitcase arrived in the camp.

In October 1941, the Germans announced the right to directly control, limit, and even prohibit Jewish employment.[12] Greatly restricted from gainful work, thousands of Jews soon became unemployed. The Germans began sending them to "work camps" in the northern part of the Netherlands. The occupiers wanted all Jews to disappear from the streets of the cities. The German authorities ordered the Jewish Council to have

1400 "unemployed" Jews ready by January 10 at 10 a.m. for transportation to these work camps.[13] Trains would be waiting for them at the Central Station of Amsterdam. This was a measure of utter cruelty because of the extremely low temperatures, strong winds, and snow. Attempts to postpone the transport failed. The recently built wooden barracks offered little protection against the cold and wind for the 1400 men in eight work camps. The letters from the men in the camps to wives and children at home testify to an intense longing to be re-united with their loved ones. The writers of these letters did not suspect that in about ten months they would indeed be re-united with their families in Poland to die in the gas chamber of a concentration camp.[14]

In January 1942 mass relocation of Jews throughout the Netherlands began. On Saturday, January 17, the Jewish Sabbath, the Nazis announced widely that all Jews throughout the Netherlands had to move to Amsterdam. Upon arrival in Amsterdam, they were required to live in restricted areas.

Jewish people became ever more aware of their impending extermination. To avoid immediate danger many single Jewish people in Amsterdam, a city which the Germans used to call *"die Judenstadt der Niederlanden,"* married non-Jewish partners, sometimes just *pro forma*. But on March 25, 1942, the *Het Joodsche Weekblad (The Jewish Weekly)* announced that from then on "marriage and sexual intercourse [by Jews] with non-Jews was forbidden." [15]

Beginning on April 27, 1942, all Jews had to wear the Jewish Star in public. On a yellow piece of cloth a six-pointed star (the David's star) was outlined in black, and inside the star the word *"Jood"* appeared in quasi-Jewish letters. Every Jew would get three of those stars, which were to be sown on the left side of their clothing above the heart.[16]

By this time protest and resistance were growing rapidly. A boy of fourteen seated himself in the bus next to a Jewish lady and started to talk to her. "I am glad to be able to sit next to you," he said. "I'm at the Lyceum, and my class has decided that whenever any of us meet anyone with a star we are going to keep them company, so that they won't feel so lonely." [17] Others lifted their hats when greeting people with a star. Some would give the star-people the right of the way. One illegal paper printed some 300,000 yellow paper stars with the heading "Jew and non-Jew are one." In Deventer many students wore imitation yellow stars with the words "Protestant" or "Roman Catholic." All of this irritated the occupying authorities immensely and made the relationship between the Germans and the Dutch even more strained.

This period can well be illustrated by the words of Dr. J. Hemelrijk describing the graduation ceremony of the Jewish Lyceum in Amsterdam:

The shadow of death hung heavily over the first graduation ceremony (it was also the last) at my school. Girls over the age of fifteen had all received orders to report for transportation to Central Station at 1 a.m. Destination unknown. All the parents knew was that they had to send their daughters out into the night, defenceless prey, never to be seen again. No one was allowed to accompany these children. The girls went, often after heart-rending domestic scenes, in the hope that by doing so they were sparing their parents. Not that they did.[18]

During the summer months of 1942 in preparation for the total deportation of the Dutch Jews, the German authorities registered (stole) most of Jews' possessions. Because not enough Jews registered for the German labor camps, the German officials ordered more raids.

III. The Deportations (July 1942–September 1943)

In July 1942 large-scale deportations of Jews began from Amsterdam. Each month several thousand Jews were transported from Amsterdam to the Westerbork transit camp located about 160 kilometers [100 miles] northeast. From Westerbork, most of these people were soon sent eastward to extermination camps in German-occupied Poland.

In July 1942, 700 Jews were arrested while walking on the streets of Amsterdam; arrests were easy because the Jews were identified by their yellow star. The SS bosses stated that the arrests were because Jews had planned a strike and because they had advised others not to go to the work camps in Germany. Some Jews refused to wear the star, and many were hiding in non-Jewish houses. The mass arrest was followed by the following announcement in *Het Joodsche Weekblad (The Jewish Weekly)*:

Some 700 Jews have been arrested in Amsterdam today. If the 4,000 called up for work-camps in Germany do not leave this week, the 700 now detained will be sent to a concentration camp in Germany.[19]

This announcement was followed by another on August 6, informing the appointed Jews that all who would not go "voluntarily" to the German work camps would be arrested and transported to Mauthausen. [20] The same punishment would apply to all Jews who did not wear the star or who moved without official permission. In this way all Jews were in effect imprisoned in their own homes.

During this misery of deportations and selections much depended on the examining physicians. But even in the most miserable situations God's gift of humor can help people to cope. An apocryphal story circulated in which a Jewish doctor, who had to examine a young Jew facing likely selection for deportation, asked, "Do you have headaches?"

"No."

"Then perhaps you can't walk very well?"

"On the contrary."

"Then it must be your heart?"

"Not at all."

"In that case I will have to reject you; you must be crazy."[21]

By early 1943, after Germany proved unable to take Stalingrad in the east and anticipated a massive military build-up by the Allies in the west, it became clear that Hitler eventually would lose the war. But even as the signs of his final defeat increased, German persecution of Jews also increased.

During this time the German governors, headed by Nazi commissioner Arthur Seyss-Inquart, planned the sterilization of all remaining Jews. This time the churches protested by issuing a statement: "Sterilization does violence to divine commandments and to human justice. It is the ultimate consequence of an anti-Christian and life-destroying racial doctrine, of overweening arrogance...."[22]

Many doctors made excuses for not performing the operation. It is reported that Dr. E. W. P. Mayer, the SS physician in charge of the sterilization program, "closed his eyes on 'hundreds of occasions' when Jews turned up with doubtful certificates signed by Dutch doctors."[23]

By May 1943 Germany was much in need of working people. So many soldiers were on the fronts that the war factories could not produce enough. Because all German requests for more workers were not answered sufficiently (even though some historians estimate that during the early war years more than half a million Dutch men were working in Germany), the governing forces decided to call back all prisoners of war of the 1940 invasion in order to put them to work in Germany. This measure greatly disturbed the Dutch population and led to a general strike in April and May of 1943.[24] As in February 1941, the May 1943 strike was smothered in blood.

One of the results, however, was that the resistance movement grew more rapidly. Soon there was an "illegal" Council of Resistance coordinating a number of resistance organizations and preparing for the day of liberation. The *Landelijke* (National) organization (L.O.), a non-violent organization, helped the 350,000 people who had gone into hiding. The group provided rationing cards to all those people. The National Knock Teams (L.K.P.) raided various distribution offices to obtain rationing cards.

The raids came to an end by September 29, just before the Jewish New Year. Asscher and Cohen were deported to Westerbork, and soon the Jewish Council ceased to exist. This was supposed to be the end of Dutch Jewry.

Part IV. The Extermination (1942–1945)

The extermination of Dutch Jews took place in Germany and in German-occupied Poland in the concentration and death camps. Most of the Dutch Jews were gassed at Auschwitz or at Sobibor. The Nazis were quite "successful" in this final phase. Presser characterizes what happened to the Dutch Jews during World War II as follows: "Those murdered on arrival [at the camps] are counted by the hundred thousand; those put to work by the ten thousand; those who returned by the hundred; and those who came forward to tell their tale in tens." [25] Of approximatly 150,000 Dutch Jews, about 110,000 did not survive the war. The Jews suffered far more than any other segment of the Dutch population.

Presser records the memories related by a woman who suffered and survived:

Every night, the past takes possession of me. I am helplessly delivered over to an irresistible force, and carried back to a place I would give anything to banish from my memory. Down to the least detail, I keep reliving a life that had really ceased to be any kind of life at all. Often it is as if I were moving through a painting by Hieronymus Bosch, a canvas peopled with fearsome monsters. I behold men and women caught in the jaws of winged horrors. The horizon is invariably hidden behind a red veil of smoke and flame.... I am pursued by visions of impenetrable clouds of smoke, which press in upon me until I cannot breathe. And then I become part and parcel of them. With all my powers, I endeavor to resist the fatal embrace, but try as I will I cannot free myself. And then, when I finally do manage to open my eyes, I can still see the dark grey wisps of smoke creeping along the walls, just as they used to rise up day and night from the chimneys, our only way out of the camp. The petty gods, who had been set over us as guards, had left us no illusions about that. Whenever, on the way to work, we would pass the crematorium, they would make us stop, and, pointing to the smoke, they would say: 'I don't know why we have to waste our time on you. Any day now, you'll be up the chimney with the rest.' And the burning of the corpses never ceased, night or day. Always the sky was fouled by an oily cloud that filled the whole horizon, covering the sorrow-stricken barracks that were our whole world. This smoke cast a pall over everything we did, until the world we had left seemed infinitely remote and unattainable.[26]

Notes

1 Jacob Presser. *The Destruction of the Dutch Jews*, trans. Arnold Pomerans (New York: E. P. Dutton & Co., Inc., 1969). With permission of the publisher, my quotations are taken from the English text. This book was first published in Holland by Staatsuitgeverij, 's-Gravenhage under the title Ondergang. Dr. Jacob Presser was Professor of History at the University of Amsterdam. A Jew, he survived the Holocaust. He also wrote *De Nacht der Girondijnen*, the novel of which "The Westerbork Train" later in this book is an excerpt. I have also consulted Louis DeJong's *Het Koninkrijk der Nederlanden in de Tweede Wereldoorlog (The Kingdom of the Netherlands during the Second World War)*, 's-Gravenhage: Martinus Nijhoff, 1969–88. This book has become the standard textbook of the history of the Netherlands 1940-1945.

2 Presser, p. 11.

3 Presser, p. 9. Many Jewish graves bear the dates May 15 and 16, 1940.

4 The event is mentioned only in the original Dutch edition of Presser's book, *Ondergang*, p. 71.

5 Presser, p. 51.

6 Presser, p. 51. Presser adds that the German soldiers and the *Grüne* (Green) Police officers were especially happy to strike the faces of people wearing eyeglasses.

7 Presser, p. 54.

8 Presser, p. 57.

9 Presser, p. 47.

10 Presser, p. 58.

11 Presser, pp. 83ff.

12 Presser, pp. 88ff.

13 Presser, pp. 98ff.

14 Presser, p. 111.

15 Presser, p. 116.

16 Presser, pp. 118ff.

17 Presser, p. 125.

18 Presser, p. 142.

19 Presser, p. 144.

20 Presser, p. 155.

21 Presser, p. 108.

22 Presser, p. 201. Dr. Jan Koopmans, who drafted this statement, was murdered in 1945.

23 Presser, p. 199.

24 For more information about the May strike, see the chapter "My War Years" later in this book.

25 Presser, p. 494.

26 Presser, pp. 494-495; quoting Greet van Amstel, *Den Vaderland Getrouwe,* p. 160.

chapter five

IN SEARCH OF AN ANSWER: *WHERE WAS GOD?*

The Holocaust confronts us with the age-old agonizing problem of suffering. Where was God when people were suffering and murdered in death camps such as Auschwitz?

The Bible tells about Job who frantically sought an answer to his suffering, an almost complete deprivation of all that made his life worthwhile. In the deep despair and pain of his aching body and tormented mind, he exclaimed:

"Why did I not perish at birth,
      and die as I came from the womb?" (Job 3:11, NIV)

His friends were of little help. They followed their straightforward, easy theology, a theology that maintained that because God is just, God cannot do any injustice. This led to the conclusion that Job's suffering must be because of something he did wrong, some evil that deserved God's punishment. They urged Job to confess and pray for forgiveness. But Job at first refused, declaring himself not guilty. Later, after God spoke to him out of the storm, challenging Job's questions and answering them in ways that Job had not expected, Job is silenced (Job 40).

The poets and prophets of old Israel, however, did not hesitate to speak up to God. Apparently the notion of covenant gave them permission as one partner to call the other one to render an explanation of his actions.

The writer of Psalm 42 lamented:

    As the deer pants for streams of water,

so my soul pants for you, O God.
My soul thirsts for God, for the living God.
    When can I go and meet with God? ....
I say to God my Rock,
    "Why have you forgotten me?
Why must I go about mourning,
    oppressed by the enemy?"
My bones suffer mortal agony
    as my foes taunt me,
saying to me all day long,
    "Where is your God?"   (Psalm 42:1-2, 9-10, NIV)

David opened his 22nd Psalm with the bitter complaint:

My God, my God, why have you forsaken me?
    Why are you so far from saving me,
        so far from the words of my groaning?
O my God, I cry out by day, but you do not answer,
    by night, and am not silent. (Psalm 22:1-2, NIV)

Though David is not silent, he finds that God is silent.

In the deep despair and darkness of his crucifixion, Jesus echoed David's words when he cried out "*Eloi, Eloi, lama sabachthani?*"— which means, "My God, my God, why have you forsaken me?" (Mark 15:34, NIV)

The question "where is God?" or "where was God?" becomes painful when God seems to be hidden or when God does not answer, and hurts especially when God's enemies are doing well. Then a heartbroken child of God wonders how God can let this happen. The poet Asaph expressed his envy of the wicked in the midst of his suffering:

For I envied the arrogant
    when I saw the prosperity of the wicked.
They have no struggles;
    their bodies are healthy and strong. (Psalm 73:3-4, NIV)

"Where is God now?" we ask in our suffering. We cannot help asking this question again and again. Perhaps we are asking the wrong question.

We are so used to the idea that God, the Almighty One, is always available to help us as soon as we call upon Him. We think that God is to be there *for* us, but the Bible reveals that God is there *with* us. He is with us in our suffering. Our God is a suffering God.

Dietrich Bonhoeffer experienced God's presence in prison in a wonderful way. In a letter dated July 16, 1944, he wrote:

"God allows himself to be edged out of the world and on to the cross. God is weak and powerless in the world, and that is exactly the way, the only way, in which He can be with us and help us.... Only a suffering God can help."[1]

The Dutch theologian K. H. Miskotte wrote: "A person cannot find the answer to his questions, but he may find deliverance out of his questions, a deliverance out of his despair and dark loneliness, also a deliverance out of his human answers." [2]

In Clara Asscher-Pinkhof's poem "The Call of the Dead Children," a dead child tells us:

But now I am dead, now I am free...

We go to the nations with our accusation.

They must listen to us, for we are dead.[3]

There are no answers, and yet there are so many aspects to the question of God's presence in or absence from Auschwitz. One of these is certainly the agony of the suffering of *El Shaddai*, the Almighty One.

Steven T. Katz in his *Post-Holocaust Dialogues: Critical Studies in Modern Jewish Thought* wrestled with the meaning of the entire body of modern Jewish thought. In doing this, Katz had to deal with the Holocaust because it has had such a deep influence on the spiritual condition of contemporary Jewry.[4]

Katz listed several Jewish responses to the Holocaust:

1. The Holocaust is like all other tragedies. It raises the difficulty of theodicy and the problem of evil, but it does not significantly change or add anything to the dilemma.

2. The classical Jewish theological doctrine of punishment for sins, which evolved in response to earlier national calamities, can also be ap-

plied to the Holocaust. Because Israel was sinful, Auschwitz was her just retribution.

3. The Holocaust is the ultimate in vicarious atonement. The "suffering servant" described by the prophet Isaiah is Israel, who suffers and atones for the sins of others. Some die so that others might live.

4. The Holocaust, like the sacrifice of Isaac, is a test of faith.

5. The Holocaust is an instance of the temporary eclipse of God. It is a time when God is inexplicably absent or chooses to turn away.

6. The Holocaust is proof that God is dead. If God exists, then God would surely have prevented Auschwitz. Because God did not prevent Auschwitz, God does not exist.

7. The Holocaust as the enormity of human evil is the price mankind has to pay for human freedom. Auschwitz reflects human imperfection; it does not relate to God's existence or perfection.

8. The Holocaust is revelation, a call for Jewish affirmation. From Auschwitz comes the command: Jews, survive!

9. The Holocaust is an inscrutable mystery like all of God's ways. Beyond human understanding, this mystery demands faith and silence.[5]

Reading through these nine options, one faces the question: what would be *my* response to the Holocaust? Is God present in history? Is there some divine plan behind the history of which we are part? Beyond what we see in history, is there also something that we cannot see? In other words, is there room for God's providence?

Perhaps more than any others, Emil Fackenheim has struggled with the problem of God's providence. For him the question "Where was God when we were dying and murdered in Auschwitz?" became a big stumbling block in understanding the Jewish experience. Why did it happen? Why did some survive but many more perish? Why is there always a "remnant" in God's or history's dealings with the Jewish people? Other nations have disappeared, but the Jews are still here, even after six million of them were killed.

Looking back into Jewish history, Fackenheim observed:

"[N]o contemporary Jewish historian at the time of the destruction of the First or the Second Temple could have fully understood the world-historical significance of that event, if only because, in the midst of the crisis, he was not yet on the other side of it. We, too, are in the midst of the contemporary crisis, and hence unable fully to understand it."[6]

In reflecting on Auschwitz, Fackenheim formulated what he "boldly term[ed] a 614th commandment," in addition to the 613 commandments which are intended to regulate the daily life of the Jewish people: *the authentic Jew of today is forbidden to hand Hitler yet another, posthumous victory."*[7] One of the implications of this 614th commandment, according to Fackenheim, is that we are "forbidden...to deny or despair of God, however much we may have to contend with him or with belief in him, lest Judaism perish." [8]

In "The 614th Commandment" Fackenheim also asked whether it is possible to come up with a response to Auschwitz that goes further than just a commitment to survival:

"[C]an we confront the Holocaust, and yet not despair? Not accidentally has it taken twenty years for us to face this question, and it is not certain that we can face it yet. The contradiction is too staggering, and every authentic escape is barred. *For we are forbidden to turn present and future life into death, as the price of remembering death at Auschwitz. And we are equally forbidden to affirm present and future life, at the price of forgetting Auschwitz."*[9]

For Fackenheim there was darkness and despair for as long as twenty years. It was impossible, it seemed, to make sense out of Auschwitz. What happened there presented this dilemma: If there was a God, Auschwitz could not have happened; or, if Auschwitz happened, there is no God. If God is, He is silent, not present, not active.

Fackenheim wondered whether he, like Martin Buber, should accept the image of the eclipse of God. [10]

Would we [like Job] be able to say that the question of Auschwitz will be answered in any sense whatever in case the eclipse of God were ended and He appeared to us? An impossible and intolerable question. Less than three months later this purely hypothetical question had become actual, when at Jerusalem the threat of total annihilation gave way to a sudden salvation, atheists spoke of miracles, and hardboiled Western reporters resorted to biblical images."[11]

The six-days war of 1967 reversed the position of Israel. Annihilation gave way to victory. The events of May and June 1967 "cast into clear relief the whole as yet unassimilated fact of an embattled, endangered, but nevertheless free Jewish state, emerging from ashes and catastrophe."[12]

Emil Fackenheim's thinking, moving from Auschwitz to the victory of 1967 and from the victory of 1967 back to Auschwitz, is like a bridge between opposite shores. Was God there? Emil Fackenheim's answer moves from "no" to "yes," and in the end "yes" wins. When he says we are "forbidden...to deny or despair of God...lest Judaism perish,"[13] it almost seems that Fackenheim's theodicy must serve his Judaism, rather than serve his affirmation of faith in the presence of God.

Fackenheim ends his essay "Jewish Faith and the Holocaust: A Fragment" with this statement:

"It is solely because of this connection of the events of May and June [1967] with Auschwitz that a Jew must both tremble and rejoice. He must tremble lest he permit any light after Auschwitz to relieve the darkness of Auschwitz. He must rejoice, lest he add to the darkness of Auschwitz. Rejoicing after Auschwitz and because of Auschwitz, the Jew must be a Jew, *Am Yisrael Chai* ("the people Israel, alive"), a witness to the world, preparing a way for God."[14]

One of my Christian friends, the late Rev. J. Overduin, who survived Dachau as a political prisoner, expressed in the title of his book *Hel en Hemel van Dachau* (*Hell and Heaven of Dachau*) the same polarity of feelings while being imprisoned in the concentration camp.[15]

Where was God when we were in Auschwitz? Is there, was there, an answer? In the concentration camp all theological questions seem to recede, yielding to the intense concentration on survival from one day to the next.

In her recent book *And Peace Never Came*, Elisabeth M. Raab describes her experiences in Auschwitz. Born in born in Hungary in 1921, she was deported to Auschwitz with her mother, father, and daughter in 1944. More than half a million Hungarian Jews went to that concentration camp. Of her family she alone survived and was liberated by the Americans in 1945. After telling about the brutal treatment she and others received upon arrival at Auschwitz, she describes her first night there:

"After what seems like an endless march, we stop at a long barracks with an open latrine along one side. We are kicked and hit through the narrow door....

A hoarse shouting silences everyone. I can't actually see her through the endless rows of women, but I hear a woman's crude screaming in broken Hungarian coming from the front. Somewhat relieved that we speak a common language, I expect a few soothing words.

"You know where you are?" she yells. "You are in Birkenau-Auschwitz. No one has ever gone out from this place alive. You will all croak here. Ladies and misses don't exist here. There are no dining rooms, no bedrooms, no bathrooms, no running water. The latrines are outside. Don't dare use them before morning. If you dare to go out after dark you'll be shot dead. Sit down where you are. You sleep where you are. There is no supper. Sit down, you imbeciles."

Bewildered, we wonder where to put ourselves.... There is no room, but somehow I manage to kneel and squeeze my feet under me. I close my eyes while it is getting darker and fold my hands for my evening prayer, as I have done every night of my life. I begin to murmur my first intimate words, "My God, King in heaven...." There, I stop. I take my hands apart. Resolutely. I have reached a watershed. I have lost my faith. I feel I will never pray again."[16]

Elisabeth Raab did not wonder about whether God was still there in Auschwitz or whether God had left or was dead. Instead, she turned to herself. She examined only her own, deep feelings. Rather than saying "God is dead," she confesses, "My faith is dead." Her answer to the Holocaust is not *objective*, but *subjective*. Whereas scholars like Emil Fackenheim look around them in every direction to find an answer to their need for the presence of God, Elisabeth Raab looked inside her soul to see whether there was any faith left. Others turned outward, but she turned inward.

When I visited Mrs. Raab in 1999, I asked her whether she had re-discovered her faith. She replied that on the Sabbath evenings she lights the candles, but she does not pronounce the blessing. Occasionally she attends services in the synagogue. When she recognizes certain melodies from her childhood, they bring back memories from a long past. "But," she said, "I was educated perhaps more Hungarian than Jewish." It seems that Elisabeth Raab is as close to being "at peace" with her faith as she can hope to be. "That God allowed the Holocaust to happen," she stated, "is a mystery. But then God himself is a mystery."[17]

She and others survive, longing to see the end of the brutality and the possibility of making a new life for themselves after their release. Some long to experience the moment when the roles will change: victims become victors and vice versa. But surviving the Holocaust means more than an opportunity for revenge. It also provides an invitation to find in all our human misery some interplay with moments of God's mercy and help. Even the darkness of Auschwitz was not able to extinguish every ray of hope. The cry of anguish: "My God, my God, why have you forsaken me? Why are you so far from saving me...?" (Psalm 22:1, NIV) remained not unanswered in the end. God saved some of his people *through* death from further suffering, others *from* death for showing the world God's saving presence in history.

My friend and co-author, Dr. Jerzy Tadeusz Pindera, a member of the Roman Catholic Church, observed:

"You asked the question *Where was God?* but you did not answer it. I guess you cannot answer the question. Neither can I. During my five years in the concentration camp I had many dark moments. There was no end in sight and survival seemed almost impossible. Yet I am here, but many others are not. Why I? Why not they? I don't know.

This is my answer. I have a dog and when I give him a simple command, he obeys. But when I ask him to do something more difficult as, for example, to help me in a scientific experiment, he is lost. So it is with God and me. I understand his commands and the gospel, but matters of his government and his presence in our suffering are too difficult for me. So I believe, but I cannot answer your question.

Pindera's conversation reminded me of an often used illustration: We see only the backside of the tapestry God is weaving; we see threads of different colors, but no pattern. We cannot see it now, but later we will when we see the other side of His work of art.

Where was God when His people were suffering and dying in Auschwitz, Dachau and many other places? Yes, I did not answer my question. I cannot. For there is no easy, logical, propositional, scientific, convincing answer. Yet, faith assures me: God was there. God suffered there. God is still here. This is hardly a theological answer to the problem, but it shows the direction in which believers always have sought their answer. Many testify: "I found it."

Several years ago, Clara Asscher-Pinkhof wrote *Sterrekinderen,* translated to English as *Star Children.* In it she describes some star children who survived long enough to hear the words "Take off your star." Many more, however, perished. Clara remembers these as "the crowds of star children who did not live long and happily, whose stars were torn off by God himself and placed among the other stars in the heavens, as eternal evidence."[18]

Evidence, one might say, of the fact that God was and is still there. Imagine one million little stars! Pharaoh's murder of the Israelite children in Egypt described in *Exodus* and Herod's murder of the Bethlehem boys in the *Gospel of Matthew* are far overshadowed by the Holocaust. But just as darkness cannot ultimately overcome the light, all of these children and dear ones of God shine on, like the stars in God's universe, forever.

Notes

1 Dietrich Bonhoeffer, *Letters and Papers from Prison,* edited by Eberhard Bethge, translated by Reginald H. Fuller (New York: The Macmillan Company, 1953), pp. 219-220.

2 Quoted by William R. Van der Zee, *Wie heeft daar woorden voor?* trans. Gerard M. Verschuuren, *Deliver Us from Evil: Is Something Wrong Between*

God and Me? (North Andover, MA: Genesis Publishing Company, 1996), p. 57.

3 Clara Asscher-Pinkof, *Danseres Zonder Benen,* 17th edition ('s-Gravenhage: Leopold U.M., 1984), p. 300.

4 Steven T. Katz, *Post-Holocaust Dialogues: Critical Studies in Modern Jewish Thought* (New York: New York University Press, 1983), p. xiii.

5 Katz, p. 144. In 1986 I conducted a small-scale survey, using Katz's 9 options. Of the 27 questionnaires I received back, 17 were completed by Jewish students, 7 were completed by people ranging in age from 37 to 70 and representing a variety of occupations, and 3 were completed by persons who did not mention their age. Of the 27, 26 were Jews. The non-Jewish person was a Presbyterian. There was also a variety in adherence to the Jewish faith. Two of those who filled out the questionnaire observed some major Jewish holidays, 8 observed them all, and a remarkable 15 attended synagogue worship services every Sabbath and called themselves "obser- vant" or "orthodox." Two did not answer this part of the questionnaire.

I presented the following abbreviated version of Katz's nine statements:

1. The holocaust raises the problem of evil, but does not substantially alter the dilemma.

2. Israel is sinful and Auschwitz is her just retribution.

3. Israel is the "suffering servant" of Isaiah; Israel atones for the sins of others.

4. The Holocaust is a test of our faith.

5. The Holocaust is an instance of the temporary "Eclipse of God."

6. The Holocaust proves that "God is dead."

7. The Holocaust is the maximization of human evil; the Holocaust re- flects ignominiously on man; it does not touch God's existence.

8. The Holocaust is revelation. The 614th command: Jews, survive!

9. The Holocaust is an inscrutable mystery.

Summary of Responses to Katz's Nine Statements about the Holocaust

	strongly agree	agree	agree mildly	disagree mildly	disagree	strongly disagree	Total
1.	1	2	0	2	10	11	26
2.	0	0	0	0	6	21	27
3.	0	2	2	0	10	12	26
4.	1	2	5	1	7	10	26
5.	1	2	1	1	8	11	24
6.	0	1	1	0	8	17	27
7.	20	7	0	0	0	0	27
8.	8	8	6	1	2	1	26
9.	3	4	4	3	4	9	27

All rejected the idea that the Holocaust was God's punishment for Israel's sins. All accepted that the Holocaust proves how evil humans can become. All respondents wanted to leave God out of the picture. Also the idea that Israel was the suffering servant was strongly rejected.

On the other hand, 25 out of the 27 did not want to say "God is dead." Does this show that the Jewish people, younger ones as well as and older ones, believe in God or believe that there is a God, but are not sure about God's presence in their lives or in history? In this respect they seem not to differ substantially from the average Canadian or American.

One respondent added comments: "The Holocaust does not demand silence, but that we remember what happened so that it does not happen again" and "just as God's existence cannot be proven, it cannot be disproved." Another added: "God has set us up with all we need to survive, but people have a free will and God rarely interferes with the course of history as determined by mankind."

6 Emil L. Fackenheim, "The 614th Commandment," *The Jewish Thought of Emil Fackenheim* (Detroit: Wayne State University Press, 1987), p. 157. Born in 1916 in Halle, Germany, Fackenheim was a prisoner in the Sachsenhausen concentration camp, near Berlin, November 1938–February 1939; after that he soon left Germany

("Reminiscences: From Germany to Canada," *Ibid.*, pp. 349-353).

7 Fackenheim, "The 614th Commandment," p. 159.

8 Fackenheim, "The 614th Commandment," p. 160.

9 Fackenheim, "The 614th Commandment," p. 159. The italics have been added by Fackenheim.

10 Cf. S. T. Katz's fifth response. Katz wrote that the image of the eclipse of God is appealing. It seems to explain that God is still there, though we cannot see Him. God is obscured or is hidden behind a cloud of darkness. It indicates a time when God is inexplicably absent or unaccountably chooses to turn away from history (*Post-Holocaust Dialogues*, p. 144). But even this explanation is ambiguous. God being God, can He be absent or even choose to be absent?

Like all theodicies this one does not seem convincing. According to Katz, the eclipse of God requires explanation because it is a metaphor that hides more than it reveals. (p. 217).

If God was not present in Auschwitz, what kind of God is He, being not omnipresent? Or, if He was present as He is supposed to be, what kind of God is He if He does not interfere with the darkness of evil and if He is not moved by compassion?

11 Fackenheim, "Jewish Faith and the Holocaust: A Fragment," in *The Jewish Thought of Emil Fackenheim* (Detroit: Wayne State University Press, 1987), pp. 165–166. The words within the brackets are also Fackenheim's.

12 Fackenheim, "Jewish Faith and the Holocaust: A Fragment," p. 166.

13 Fackenheim, "The 614th Commandment," p. 160.

14 Fackenheim, "Jewish Faith and the Holocaust: A Fragment," p. 167.

15 The book was translated by Harry der Nederlanden and published by Paideia Press, Jordan, Ontario. The change of the original title from "Hell and Heaven" to "Faith and Victory" regrettably eliminated the polarity of Overduin's concentration camp experiences, the conflict between "God was there" and "God was not there," Fackenheim's "yes" and "no."

16 Elisabeth M. Raab, *And Peace Never Came*, volume 3 in the Life

Writing Series edited by Marlene Kadar (Waterloo, Ontario: Wilfrid Laurier University Press, 1997), pp. 36–37. In June 1999, my wife and I had the wonderful opportunity to visit Raab, then age seventy-eight. Roses were blooming in the yard of her beautiful Toronto residence, where she felt very much at home.

17 Raab's response here is very similar to Katz's response number 9 above.

18 Clara Asscher-Pinkhof, *Star Children* (Detroit: Wayne State University Press, 1986), p. 255.

part two

SURVIVORS
OF THE HOLOCAUST

chapter six

MY NARROW ESCAPE

THE STORY OF CLARA ASSCHER-PINKHOF

From Her Autobiography, *Danseres Zonder Benen*
[*Ballerina Without Legs*]

I. Introduction

Clara Asscher-Pinkhof (1896-1984) in her autobiography, Danseres
Zonder Benen [Ballerina Without Legs], *describes her personal struggles
during World War II interwoven with the fate of many Dutch Jews.*

*She was married to Orthodox Rabbi Avraham Asscher, who died in
1926. She was then a young widow, the mother of six children, and remained single the rest of her life. Though often insecure and lonely, she
gave her children a background of Jewish consciousness, mutual care,
humor, and love. By writing children's stories she succeeded in augment-
ing her meager pension.*

Her excellent book Danseres Zonder Benen *was first published in
1966 and reprinted 20 times in the Netherlands. Regrettably, it has not
yet been translated into English. With the permission of the author's daughter, Mrs. Fieke Langer-Asscher, I translated the following portions of the
book* [1] *and The Star, a chapter later in this book.*

II. I Moved to Amsterdam

After the summer vacation, when the Jewish children, filled with hope and expectation, had returned to their new classes, the order came: Jewish children were allowed to attend classes only in Jewish schools; there they could be instructed only by Jewish teachers, and Jewish teachers were no longer allowed to teach non-Jewish children.

In the *Het Joodsche Weekblad (the Jewish Weekly)* I read on a Sunday night that in Amsterdam, where the major part of the Jewish population crowded together, an acute need for Jewish teachers had developed.

Instantly, I understood what this meant for me. I was a teacher with credits for being a principal,[2] and I was a Jew. I did not have the right to stay in Groningen when I was needed in Amsterdam.[3]

About fifteen minutes later, I let my letter, addressed to the Jewish congregation in Amsterdam, slide down into the mailbox. Within minutes I vacated my place as mother of a family (only two of the six were at home any more). I had to go, immediately.

The last night that I slept in my own bed I had a strange dream:

I was seated at an open drawer of my desk and I touched all kinds of things which were kept there. Behind me, a door was opened and a doll, dressed in men's clothing, was pushed in. I knew that this doll had to represent Avraham, my deceased husband. From the door opening came a voice—and I knew whose voice it was—which said: "You did all things well with the children and all the rest—but you have forgotten the death clothes."

I shouted: "Death clothes? But I don't even know what death clothes look like!"

The doll was clothed in men's clothes, not in death clothes, since I did not know what death clothes were.

I woke up, tired of my shouting. Suddenly I understood that Avraham had become a doll and that I had not stopped playing with him; I had forgotten to give him his death clothes.

Then the movers came and they took away all the things with which I had played all those years.[4]

III. In Amsterdam: Increasing Discrimination and Isolation

Slowly, slowly the anguish around us increased. Slowly, slowly holes appeared in the classroom: empty seats of girls who were present yesterday but had been taken away during the night. To fill out the register of attendance became more painful every day.

The Jewish star became compulsory; what this was going to mean, we did not realize. Children walked around, proud of the star on their coat. At first you were reverently greeted on the street by the non-Jewish people. Men took off their hat for this yellow emblem with the word "Jew" on it in mock-Hebrew letters. In the streetcar people stood up to offer you their place. But there were too many Jewish stars around to keep on taking off your hat: people got used to them. Soon Jews were not allowed in the streetcars any more; neither were they supposed to sit on the benches in the parks. Later they were not permitted to walk in the parks, for the parks were green and offered relaxation. So where in the world could somebody still stand up for a Jew?

Jews were not allowed to visit public concerts. They were not to listen to Aryan music produced by Aryan musicians or to be in the company of Aryan listeners. They should organize their own concerts: there were plenty of Jewish musicians and more Jewish composers than we had assumed and—in the midst of all this misery—Jews were still hungry for music.

Just a few days before the telephones were cut off, I received a call.

"Mother," said my son Elie, "brother Menachem and I have heard that you don't get so easily deported if you are married. Menachem and [his girlfriend] Tamar and Flory [my girlfriend] and I have taken out the banns. Next week we will get married."

"OK," I said. "Could you perhaps still tell me when exactly this will take place?"

So this is how it goes now when two of your boys get married. They just give you a phone call that they have been registered and next week they will be married men. Even though the civil marriage does not hold any meaning for them, next week they will be legally married men.[5]

IV. In the Schouwburg (Amsterdam City Theater)[6]

[After the marriage I felt empty]; I could not stand this.

Vacation from school, no faces of girls in front of me, girls who compelled me to think only about them.

I found a solution by offering my help for the *Schouwburg* during the nights that Jews were being assembled there for further transportation. A token on my identity card still protected me from deportation—at least as long as this would last...

It was wild, wild; even in hell it could not have been wilder than in this *schouwburg*. It was a mass of small children, sick ones, some on the plush folding chairs of the mezzanine, others in the stalls, the loges, or on the wooden benches of the gallery, others again on straw mattresses in the dirt and the dust of the hallways. People formed a slow-moving stream up and down the stairs, and on the top floor was the room in which the very sick people were brought together. But the sick room was no place for vomiting children and desperate, yelling adults. In the midst of all these people we, the few attending helpers, were working, and we developed in *one* night the instinct to feel where we were needed most.

In the midst of the stream I noticed a man: I saw clearly that he was about to fall. I moved towards him through the jostling mass of people, took his arm, and walked with him up a few steps as if we had known each other for a long time. At the top of the lower stairway, I said: "Shall we sit down?" And just as we sat down on the highest step, he fell sideways against me. He just had the time to mention his name and the name of his wife, who was sitting in a room downstairs, before he lost consciousness. I was holding him to prevent him from falling down and from being trampled by the feet of the stream of people coming up. I asked a man who was passing by to request the radio announcer to ask the wife of my patient to come to the stairway and to alarm one of the doctors.

Later that same night I walked past him from time to time, and fairly soon he regained consciousness. His heart attack, which I had recognized on the stairway, kept him for the time being from being transported.

When finally the prisoners were expelled from the building, up the dark street, where the streetcars with their few, ghostly blue lights were waiting for them, all strength would suddenly ebb away from me. We, the helpers, were not needed any more, but we still had to stay till 6 a.m., since nobody was allowed earlier on the streets.

At home, in the apartment which Fieke, my daughter, shared with me, I fell into a bottomless deep sleep: I had vacation from school—I did not have to get up.

Sometimes I wished I would never have to get up again.

It was during one of these nightly expulsions that I saw among all these heavy-loaded, pursued people a slender, stooped old Jew who was almost breaking under his burden. At the moment that I was going to help him, a towering SS-man, in green uniform, discovered him; he gave him a push and he would have fallen had not the milling crowd kept him standing. The SS-er yelled in the only language he still knew: "Hurry up, hurry!"

At that moment, in a stricture of consciousness, which caused me to forget the uselessness of my counter attack, I placed myself right in front of this big fellow and yelled: "Let go!"

The man, appalled by the fact that a woman with a star dared to yell at him, the authority, hissed voicelessly with a raised fist: "What, what?"

And before the fist came down, he roared:

"One word more and you'll see what happens."

By now I had lost all feeling for safety and proportion; the suffering in the *Schouwburg* had weakened me. I looked in that contorted, swollen face and said: "I thought you were a human being."

The fist went higher. But just before it hit me, others who had heard everything gripped me and removed me in the throng.

"Up, go up," someone hissed, "go to the sick room."

I went up against the stream of the expelled ones and I reached the hospital ward. The sick were lying there, waiting to see whether the highest deciding authority was drunk or not. I sat down next to the mattress of a semi-conscious patient and, wiping his sweaty face, I came to myself again. I understood how useless my shout had been and how despair had broken all restrictions in me; yet I also had a vague feeling of liberation.[7]

V. Sick

The long walks through the city without any means of transportation took their toll on my spine. Coming back from a visit to my parents took me many hours. I crept more than I walked. Finally. I ended up in bed. Lying down I would have to wait for being picked up.[8]

Then, one day, a girl from my class dropped by, pale and horrified.

"May I stay with you? I don't have a home any more."

(When the Gestapo had arrested the people in the home where she lived, they had not found this girl, Milie, who was hiding. Now she did not know where to go.)

"Of course, you can stay here."

"But if they find me here, and I have no special stamp on my identity card, is that not dangerous for you?"

This fourteen-year old child was exceptionally thoughtful: having no home for herself any more, she thought about the danger for me.

[We enjoyed each others company for nine days.]

Then, suddenly, my room was full with three tall, black policemen— the Dutch accomplices of the [ruling] power—three men towering high above my sickbed and above the girl whose mother I had been for nine days. They entered every house to control whether any Jews without the protecting stamp on their identity card had stayed behind.

With loud masculine voiced they asked: "Why is this child here?"

"I was her teacher. She lost her home and came to me."

"Where is your husband?"

"Dead, for seventeen years."

I did not say that during all these months my often returning thought was: "I thank God that he does not have to go through all this."

"Well, if we find him...?"

I almost smiled. Perhaps they noticed this for now they turned to the girl and commanded her to get her backpack ready as soon as possible to go along with them. Two of the men left. The third one, who himself apparently did not need any protection, stayed.

He took a chair and waited. Somewhat more friendly, he shouted to the girl in the sideroom that she should take some warm clothes along and some food. He then tried to start a talk with me.

"You know perhaps that pretty soon the protecting stamp on your identity card will not be valid any more."

Yes, I knew this. "For me it will not make much difference whether I am in a camp or here. I will find everywhere children who need me."

"Do you have children of your own?"

"I had six children, but I don't know whether I still have them."

Silence. Apparently, he wanted to change the subject. "You better accept," he started again, "that we too are victims."

"No," I said, "you are not. None of you. You could have made another choice. But this child," and I pointed to the side room, "this child is a victim, a victim of you and your people. You have taken her away."

At that moment Milie entered the room with the backpack in her hand, pale and red-eyed. In the other hand she held a necklace, which she laid down next to me on my cushion. It was a pale ivory brooch on a silken cord. "Would you keep this for me—till later. I got it from my mother."

I kept it till later. I still have it.

I put my hand on her head to give her the blessing, which I also had given along with Fieke: "like Sarah, Rebekah, Rachel and Leah" and the old priestly blessing.[9]

"I must go on," the black policeman said. "Come."

She went with him.

When they had reached the door of my room, I got my voice back. I said to this man: "I hope you soon will find a better job."

Suddenly he put his forehead against the doorpost and cried. Then the door was closed behind these two. I stayed behind, dazed.

In the evening [son] Elie dropped by, the first living being I saw after all that had happened in my room. I told him the whole story. His sorrow for Milie could not prevent him saying with triumph in his voice: "That you could do this—lying in bed and send off such a fellow, weeping."

Sorry—I could not share in his triumph. For that you would have to be young, just like Elie. I knew only that I had not been able to save Milie.[10]

VI. In Westerbork

After her recovery came the time when Clara too was deported to Westerbork. She continues her story:

So this was the deportation camp, Westerbork, on the Drentian heather.[11] Here the weeks had only six days: from Tuesday afternoon till Monday morning. On Tuesday afternoon they counted how many were left behind and with those left behind you created something that looked like life. This life went on till Monday morning when the long row of cattle cars appeared on the rails beside the camp, waiting for its weekly load of Jews condemned to death. Life came to a standstill when on Monday nights the lists of the condemned were read in the barracks: gray old people, sick ones, healthy men, women with children. That was a life which did not breathe life any more; those who were left behind were locked up in the barracks for they were not allowed to see what was happening at the rails. A puff of steam was expelled by the puffing engine, which pulled along the full cattle cars.[12]

I was called to work in the barracks for the orphans, where educators and teachers were needed because other educators and teachers had been sent away in the train. Children too were sent along but with every razzia-load other children arrived from the city: children with parents, children without parents, children with sick parents, who had to be admitted to the hospital barracks, children whose parents were lost or in hiding.

So it happened that my work after a week of peeling potatoes changed back to educating and teaching. I became again a mother, a mother of hundreds of children, tall ones and small ones.[13]

My father [both of Clara's elderly parents also had been deported to Westerbork] was given work, something that was very suitable for an eighty-year-old physician, a language connoisseur: the translation of the history of the sicknesses of the inmates of the camp, from Dutch into German. For the Germans were of the opinion that they ought to be able to check everything that happened in the hospital barracks, whether they had any expertise in that field or not. Hence they made it mandatory for Jewish physicians with expert knowledge in their specialization to explain their actions in understandable language. My father was even given a secretary to help him.

But on a Friday morning, three weeks after my parents had arrived in the camp, the secretary looked up from her work because my father had ceased to dictate. She noticed that he had lost consciousness sitting at his desk behind his papers.

He had pneumonia, the result of his breathing in of particles of straw and dust, which descended on him continuously from the bed above him.

[The next] Thursday night he was given a small room in which there were only two beds. We visited him. He said to my mother: "You have always spoiled me."

And my mother, great and honest, especially with regard to herself, answered: "Spoiled, no, but loved, yes."

The next morning we were called to the hospital. But we came just a moment too late.

We were allowed to follow him to the outer gate of the camp. The bearers of the stretcher went on to a small stone structure out of which smoke always was rising up.

The bearers returned with an empty stretcher. My father stayed there.

Years later we received an urn with ashes on which his name had been written. It was buried on a Sunday morning, one day after the Jewish nation, the nation Israel, for which he had been longing all his life, had become a reality, on the fourteenth of May 1948. He had known it from the Scriptures. God had promised: "As I have brought all this great calamity on this people, so I will give them all the prosperity I have promised them."[14]

VII. How I Got Mindeltje

In the barracks for babies and toddlers I met a frail child, light as a feather. Her name was Mindeltje. She did not weigh more than a child of two-and-a-half years because of a few pneumonias which she had successfully sustained. In fact she was four years old, but her conceited little mouth gave the impression that she was older than six.

It was not her dancing, golden, silky curls or her starry eyes which provided for this small attractive female being such a central place in my life. It was the whisper of adult people, who had not known her parents and did not have any written proof for their story: her parents were supposed to be in Israel.

I was told that her parents had left her behind in the Netherlands as a little baby. Nobody knew how it had happened that the parents escaped to Israel without their baby. This child finally ended up in a Jewish orphanage, and when this orphanage was "emptied," she had been deported to the toddlers barracks in Westerbork.[15]

VIII. Escape Possible?

One day, quite suddenly, a rumor was heard and people talked about Bergen-Belsen. This was—as people told and people believed—an exchange camp for people with a foreign passport or certificate, under the supervision of the Red Cross. There were many people with a foreign passport or certificate from countries they had never seen in their whole life but which were supposed to offer protection against the Nazis, and therefore those papers were bought for much money. And then there were also people like myself: people who had children or parents in Palestine and who, because of this, possessed a certificate. But Mindeltje, who had her parents in Palestine, did not have such a certificate. (Who could have sent her a telegram via the Red Cross?) She missed every proof that her parents were living in Palestine. The request to add her name to my certificate had been refused.

At that time a female S.S.-civil servant came to the camp to determine whether those who had foreign certificates would qualify for going to Bergen-Belsen or not. She had a typical sharp voice and talked in a curt way, characteristic of the powerful; nothing escaped her sharp vision.

Since my name began with an A, I was one of the first ones to appear before her in her barracks. She asked me to put my camp card and my certificate on her desk, she examined them and then looked me over from head to toe.

"Your husband?"

"Dead."

"When?"

"1926."

She made a note.

"Children?"

"I had six, but I don't know whether I still have them."

Louder: "Where are they?"

I shrugged my shoulders. Thanks to God, I did not know where they were. I knew it from Roza, but she was out of reach.

"Are you interested in being sent to Bergen-Belsen?"

"If it is on my way to Palestine, yes."

"Is your name Asscher related to the diamond-king Asscher?"

"My deceased husband was his nephew. But I myself have never possessed one diamond."

What I did not know then but understood later was that the Nazis, in their search for disappeared and disappearing diamonds, needed hostages related to the diamond world.

"O.K. Being a relative of the diamond-king, you may stay here in Westerbork."

"But I want to go to Palestine."

With a gesture she told me to be silent. My case was finished. But suddenly I decided that even if my case was finished, the case of Mindeltje was not.

"There is still something else about which I would like to talk to you," I started, somewhat hurriedly, "I work in the barracks of the orphans and I found there a four-year-old child, Mindeltje, whose parents live in Palestine. I want to take that child on my certificate to Palestine in order to give her back to her parents."

The absurdity of my request must have touched her sense of humor: a wooden smile flew over her face. "But I told you: you can stay quietly here. Then you can also quietly continue to care for that child."

"Quietly care"— and then wait every Monday night to hear whether Mindeltje's name was on the list? I returned to my barracks and looked in on the toddlers room, where Mindeltje was playing, unaware of what was happening around her.

But the SS-woman had a strong memory. That afternoon a notice came for Mindeltje to appear in person before the Mighty one.

When our turn had come, I placed the small, pale child in front of the woman, and she reacted, before she realized it, as every mother would: "Poor thing."

I said, "this is the child about which I talked this morning; the child I would like to give back to her parents."

The woman made a rapid recovery from her moment of tenderness. She said, "but I told you, didn't I, that you can stay here quietly to care for this child?"

Then there was a short in me. I lost my composure for one moment and I shouted loud and fast: "No. This child has no time to wait. You know this just as well as I. She has to be returned to her parents, and I am the one who will do this!"

Something happened. It had to do with being a woman, with being human. It had something to do with the policeman who had cried against my door post. The woman looked me straight in the face, and then she looked down on Mindeltje, who looked in amazement to her aunt Clara whom she had never seen so upset. Then the short sharp voice said slowly and was toned down: "O.K. The child will be added to the exchange list."

In the evening two notes were brought to our barracks: one for Mindeltje, one for me. They read:

"*Clara Asscher-Pinkhof is eligible for the exchange camp in Bergen-Belsen. The child Mindel F. belongs to her.*"

"*Mindel F. is eligible for the exchange camp in Bergen-Belsen. She belongs to Clara Asscher-Pinkhof.*"[16]

It took still many weeks before the transport of a passenger-train left the camp. At one time, as in a mirage, such a passenger-train appeared on the rails on which usually only cattle trains were standing. It stood there for a day and a night and then it departed, empty.

During these many weeks Mindeltje began to understand that she belonged to *tante* (aunt) Clara, that she belonged to *someone*. She asked with her high voice: "Am I now of you?"

("Careful now!" I said to my longing self. "You got this child for her parents, not for yourself.")

"On the way, you are mine."

"On the way, to what?"

"To Palestine." (Fool, fool, Bergen-Belsen is not Palestine—not even on the way to it!)

"And in Palestine?"

"Then you are from your Pappy and Mommy."

Silence.

"In Palestine, do I go in the men's barracks by my Pappy or in the women's barracks with my Mommy?"

"No, you go to live in a little house for all three of you."

She asked patiently further: "Yes, but is it a men's house or a women's house?"

O God, why doesn't she know what a family is?[17]

IX. In Bergen-Belsen

The chapter in which Clara Asscher-Pinkhof describes her stay in the concentration camp Bergen-Belsen is titled: Diepste Diepte, [Deepest Depth]. *Rightly so. Clara tells:*

No, Bergen-Belsen was not Palestine and also not on the way there.

We knew it when we, stiffened, wriggled ourselves out of the railroad cars in which we had been sitting during the night, shaken by jerks and starts, moving forward for a little while and standing still during long hours, buried under the luggage, which had been thrown inside. The loaves of bread, sent along from Westerbork, which had caused us to make hopeful predictions, had traveled along in a special luggage room, for in the cars themselves they would not have remained untouched; now they were lying in a pile on the ground of the dirty station's platform. SS-men, decorated with skeleton faces, shouted commands at us; we were herded together and then divided into groups and rows of pedestrians for the long walk from the station to the camp. The sick ones and mothers with children were pushed into a completely darkened truck. I got in that truck because Mindeltje was now my child and, even though I could hear her high, desperate voice in that crammed darkness, I could not reach her. All I could do was shout: "Mindeltje, Mindeltje, Aunt Clara is here!" But there were so many women's voices calling out the name of a child, telling that mother was there, that none of us knew whether our calls had been heard. We could only pray in our hearts that our child would not be trampled by all these feet.

Suddenly there was the saving voice of a mother who started to sing a children's song. This could be heard clearly in the midst of the hell of terrified screams—and a silence was born. Then children and mothers started to sing along; we sang one song after another until suddenly the moving darkness stood still and the back wall was opened. Not one child was trampled under the feet of the other ones.

O yes, we knew it now for sure that we were "on our way to Palestine." The cacophony of shouting and cursing in the German language made this clearer and more evident than any explanation.[18]

X. How I Lost Mindeltje

Excitement strangled our throats, those of us who had papers for Palestine. A command was announced that all Palestine-people, with their papers, their families, and belongings had to appear on the roll-call field. They had to leave their work and take up their position in rows of five. There were more than one thousand of us. My mother, my two brothers, and two brothers of Avraham, Mindeltje and I—we all belonged to this group.

The commander explained what the idea of this appeal was: there was talk about an exchange transport to Palestine. The names of those who had been elected were read. We all were on that list. Then we were sent back to our barracks—those who had not been elected in despair, the elect skeptical and doubtful.

The next day the same play took place, but now with a changed list. Names of those missing on yesterday's list were added, but other names mentioned yesterday had now been crossed out. My mother's name had been omitted.

This time the elect had to return to their barracks to pick up their possessions. When they had returned to the roll-call area, they were immediately transported further. Passing one gate, they came to an adjoining, small camp with only a few barracks.

Those who had stayed behind stood that same day on the roll-call field for a long time till it became dark. We saw this through the barbed wire fences and we wept. Among those thousands who were standing there for many hours was my mother, seventy-seven years of age.[19]

As soon as I came into the camp of the elect, I wrote a request for my mother and handed it over to the commander, who in this camp suddenly could talk to us as human beings. He promised to send it on to Berlin. I had signed the request with my full name, Asscher-Pinkhof. Much later I learned that this led to the destruction of my brothers and brothers in law and that it would have been also my destruction if not, at the very last moment, a great miracle had happened. In Berlin, the devil's kitchen, they had decided: let this one, the old woman, be set free, that we take in her place anyone who is called Asscher or Pinkhof.[20]

Weeks went by. Hardly anybody mentioned any more the exchange journey to Palestine. Yet, after five weeks, on the bright beautiful morning of the Shavuot feast[21] a special roll-call was announced in the presence of some high uniforms of mighty ones from Berlin. Now we understood why we had been separated from the larger camp.

The tension was almost unbearable when they started reading an alphabetical list of those who had to keep themselves ready for the journey that "soon" would take place. Tension increased even more when the reading of the names was interrupted because allied planes came flying over. We went back to the barracks and the high officers went into hiding in their underground shelters.

During the interruption we looked at each other terrified, for names had been omitted. My name started with an A. I had been left out.

When finally the list was completed, fifty-one names were missing. All who were called Asscher and all who were called Pinkhof, seventeen in total, had been left out. But Mindeltje was among the elect. I told her to ask the commander whether she had to travel to Palestine all by herself. There she was standing, small and fragile in front of the heavy, stout commander.

"Commander! Do I have to go all by myself to Palestine?"

The commander, confused, did not respond immediately. It was evident that he was directed by the mighty ones in Berlin.

"Commander! Tell me, do I go all alone?"

He sent her back to me, even though I was already standing, in the rows of five, with those who were to be sent back to the big camp.

"Ask," he said, "who of the women who will travel will care for her."

I lifted Mindeltje up and offered her. "Is there anyone who will care for Mindeltje during the trip?"

A few hands went up. I chose a mother who herself had small children. Mindeltje skipped happily to her. When she was standing again with the two-hundred-and-forty-nine elect, she nodded to me triumphantly,

"I am happy. I go to Palestine!"

Two-hundred-and-forty-nine. There had been three-hundred—fifty-one too many.

The commander held in his hand an official paper. "Pinkhof-DeBeer, Adèle, has been allowed to join the travelers." That was my mother, number two-hundred-and-fifty.

An SS-man was sent to the big camp to get her. There she stood, terrified, at the other side of the barbed-wire hedge. She was very small with that wide, empty roll-call field behind her.

"Do you wish to travel to Palestine?" the commander shouted.

Her eyes opened wide.

"Yes," her mouth said, but it was hardly audible.

"All your relatives will stay here."

Her head sank. Never had she been that small. It was clearly visible that she did not know anymore whether she wanted to travel to Palestine.

The commanded gave me a sign to go to the barbed wire.

"Tell her," he commanded me, "what she has to do."

I stood in front of her. Yet I had to shout, for there were many rows of barbed wire between her and me. I had to shout to my mother that she should choose life.

"You must go. It does not help us if you stay here. In Palestine you have a daughter and a granddaughter waiting for you."

She had looked at me while I spoke. Now she bent her head and said, "Yes." I turned to the commander and communicated the "yes" to him.[22]

XI. Reunited with Mindeltje

[So I returned to the main camp.] We women were driven to the showers. In nude rows of five we had to wait in the ice-cold hall in front of the showers till the women who had preceded us—in order to catch, with five or six under one shower, a few drips of warm water—came out there, wet and steaming. You noticed that each time the women looked more skeleton-like, their bones sticking out, and you suppressed the question whether you too looked like one of them. You counted by yourself how many after the previous shower had died from pneumonia. Nobody said what she noticed in someone else; if you were caught in the observation of some other person, you looked fast in another direction.

And yet, everyone of us, to one's last day, remained intensely involved in what happened in the world. Allied armies had landed in France? Could this be true? But the Allied forces never did anything, did they? Yes, it was indeed true, and the news reached the barracks of the French Jews. Women grabbed each other at the shoulders, eyes sparkling, kissed each other on both cheeks and danced, danced. Yes, it should really be true.[23]

Those who were prepared for the trip [to Palestine] and were staying in the lucky barracks[24] were still ready to go and still waiting. Finally, also the elect [from the lucky camp] were sent back to the big camp, first still free from slave labor, but after half a week also incorporated in the slavery. The doubting of the journey had increased so much that the shock of being sent back to the larger camp did not even hurt too much.

We, my brothers and I myself, could now talk again with my mother. We visited her in the barracks of the dethroned ones which was filled beyond capacity. The only hopeful sign was that those [from the smaller lucky camp] were not divided up, but stayed together.[25]

Where did all these rumors always come from? How could every time again hope flare up as a thorny bush? "They say." "They say."

It was that Wednesday night, the twenty-ninth of June, that the whispered words, "they say," "they say," notwithstanding all previous disappointments, were heard and passed on with more reliability than otherwise. "They say that there yet will be a journey to Palestine. They say that a group will leave tomorrow already."

"Most likely it will not be true."

"Good night, sleep well."

"Tomorrow we will see each other again," my mother said, "so often there have been rumors like this."

But this time it was true. In the early morning we saw the group on the small roll-call field, surrounded by backpacks, which were inspected by nervous SS-men. My youngest brother was standing on guard at the exit in the barbed wire through which the lucky ones had left the main camp. He stood there turned towards us and his back towards the lucky ones, among whom he knew our mother was. It was his task to guard and maintain the strict separation between the two kinds of Jews, the elect and the damned.

The roll-call took place in full length and all strictness. Before the SS-man appeared, the women were talking with each other, excited, tense. However, after they had discussed from all angles the question whether it would be true that we were going to Palestine or that we just would be transported to another camp, they returned to their daily remedy against the hunger, which they called "cooking." It consisted of teaching each other new recipes with many eggs, much butter, much sugar. I always had refrained from taking part in this because it did not help me, but today I said, "It does not matter to me *what* I eat, but I would like it so much that I could eat once again to my satisfaction and I also would like it very much if once again I could eat from a table properly laid."

At this moment the SS man appeared on the field and all was quiet. They stood in rows of five, the men with uncovered heads. More Allied planes than usual were flying over our field. To us it did not matter what would fall from the skies, but our guards were more concerned. They looked at the sky, heard the noise, and decided that it was too dangerous to do the roll-call.

So they sent the prisoners back to their barracks. Exhausted from a sleepless night, in which the fretting about the question whether the chosen ones would still depart for Palestine or not was interrupted by the yelling between a grandmother and her grandson, I crawled back on my pallet and fell immediately in a deep sleep. I was startled out of my rest when my name was called out in the barracks.

"Asscher-Pinkhof, Clara, has to come to the commander."

Was that I? But the commander was at the small roll-call field, wasn't he? Or had I ...?

Suddenly I was wide awake. Would I too have to come to the commander at the small roll-call field, among all the people, ready to travel, and their backpacks? Very soon I stood, in attention, facing the commander.

My mother, busy with something, did not see me standing in front of the commander. Somebody pointed me out to her, looking in my direction. My mother's eyes and mouth opened widely, but I was not supposed to make a move indicating that I had seen her.

The commander said curtly: "Asscher-Pinkhof, Clara?"

Yes, that was I.

"A few travelers dropped off. Do you have relatives in this transport?"

"Yes, my mother and my foster child."

"Do you have relatives in Palestine?"

"Yes, my daughter and my sister."

"Then you may go along. Return to your barracks, get your luggage and return immediately. It is more than time."

In later years, when I moved from one room to another in the same kibbutz, I prepared for this event days before, and the move itself took one whole day. Now I had only five minutes to gather my possessions— and I was moving from Europe to Asia—from a prison to freedom, from death to life.

It was more than time. Together with me a whole family came, just as unbelieving as I. On the list had been some very sick people and also some relatives from dying inmates. These could not go along. We had been given their places.

My mother mumbled to herself: "Still not alone."

It dawned on me that I would have to do something with my restored life. To me that was a mandate. It became a command.

Away. Through another gate, but still on that big, condemned area, called Bergen-Belsen. Along the road slaves were working, our friends whom we left behind. They were not allowed to say anything, but they held their hands together as if they were holding ours. They were so good: the only thing they could give us along was their blessing, but they themselves were condemned to stay and to die.

We were brought to an empty garage. Sitting or squatting on the earthen floor or leaning against each other, we entered the night, sometimes dozing, sometimes sleeping, and sometimes waking up with a scare, trying to understand what had happened to us and might happen later.

Then came the command: "In rows of five." It was three o'clock in the night, in the summer night of the first of July. In rows of five we walked into the night in the direction of the white barrier, which had been the uttermost border of our captivity. The barrier went up to let us pass. My mother and I, next to each other, took each other's hand.[26]

Postscript

Clara with her mother and Mindeltje arrived after ten days in Haifa. Mindeltje's parents were there to claim their child. Clara slept that first night deep and dreamless. Yes, she was back in a camp, but now in Erets Jisrael.[27] Her friend Miriam had given her a letter from daughter Rose.

Clara continues her story:

That afternoon Miriam told me that a taxicab would drive to Jerusalem and that there was a place for me. Miriam walked behind the two elderly women and me. The first gate went open, then a second one. It was only a small distance from this gate to the road where the taxi was waiting. Yet the distance was too much for me. I did not dare to cross, entering that big space.

"Come, Clara," Miriam said behind me. "Go on. You are free now."

Free. What kind of word was that? When it dawned on me, what that word meant, I started to cry so unrestrained that the driver of the taxi, to whom Miriam had pushed me gently, wept with me.

[After they arrived in Jerusalem] In a garden in front of the house, in the shadow of a tree, a young woman was sitting.

"Is that...?" I hesitated.

"Yes," my companion said, "That is Rose."

I thought, once more, anxiously: "But my own child will not recognize me."

I stood beside the car and my child said, "Mother."[28]

Notes

1 Clara's daughter wrote me that one of her mother's books was translated to English. In 1986 Wayne State University Press, Detroit, Michigan, published it as *Star Children.*

2 This certificate, called *hoofdacte* in Dutch, required one year of additional study after obtaining the certificate for teaching in elementary schools.

3 Groningen is a city in the Northeastern part of the Netherlands.

4 Clara Asscher-Pinkhof, *Danseres Zonder Benen* (17th edition; 's-Gravenhage: Leopold U.M., 1984), pp. 135-137.

5 Asscher-Pinkhof, excerpts from chapter 12, pp. 139-143.

6 The Schouwburg or the Amsterdam City Theater is the famous auditorium built by Nicolaas VanCampen, which was opened on January 3rd 1638 with the play *Gysbreght Van Aemstel,* written for this occasion by Joost VandenVondel.

7 Asscher-Pinkhof, pp. 149-153.

8 Asscher-Pinkhof, p. 173.

9 See Numbers 6:24-26 (NIV):

> The LORD bless you
> and keep you;
> the LORD make his face shine upon you
> and be gracious to you;
> the LORD turn his face toward you
> and give you peace.

10 Asscher-Pinkhof, pp. 174-177.

11 Drente is a province in the Northeastern part of the country. It is worthwhile to compare this chapter of *Danseres Zonder Benen* with the chapter titled "The Train" by Jan Presser in this book.

12 Asscher-Pinkhof, p. 182.

13 Asscher-Pinkhof, p. 185

14 Jeremiah 32:42. During the siege of Jerusalem Jeremiah is ordered by

God to buy a field, an act which symbolized the restoration which would follow the exile. Asscher-Pinkhof, pp. 193-94.

15 Asscher-Pinkhof, p. 204.

16 Emphasis added by Remkes Kooistra.

17 Asscher-Pinkhof, pp. 207-211.

18 Asscher-Pinkhof, pp. 212-13.

19 Asscher-Pinkhof, p. 232.

20 Asscher-Pinkhof, pp. 232-23.

21 *Shavuot* means Feast of Weeks, celebrated on the fiftieth day after the Passover, known as the day of Pentecost.

22 Asscher-Pinkhof, pp. 236-37.

23 Asscher-Pinkhof, pp. 239-40.

24 These lucky barracks were smaller than the others and located in a special area behind a barbed-wire fence. The prisoners there received preferential treatment and were exempt from slave labor. Clara's mother was here.

25 This meant there would still be a chance that they might travel together to Palestine.

26 Asscher-Pinkhof, pp. 244-247.

27 Erets Jisrael is Hebrew for the land, the country Israel, the land promised to Abraham, captured by Joshua, lost in captivity, and regained under Cyrus of Persia in 538 B.C.

28 Asscher-Pinkhof, pp. 268, 270.

chapter seven
EVA BROSS'S STORY

This is the story of Mrs. Eva Bross (1913-1989), which she told me one cold November night of 1988, about one year before her death.[1]

My name is Eva Bross; that is my married name. When I was born in Warsaw, Poland, my name was Emma Grimsberg. I was born on the fifth day of May in 1913. The first twenty-seven years of my life were quite normal, without major events. I was my parents' only child. My education was completed with graduation from high school. My father made his living in the wheat trade, buying and selling.

We were Jewish, but not very orthodox. Like many other Jews, we observed the major Jewish holidays. We ate kosher food and on the Sabbath day we usually went to *Shul*, the Synagogue. Thus our religious life was more observing rituals than a matter of deep, inner spirituality.

I got married in my early twenties according to our tradition. My first husband was industrious. As a factory worker, he earned enough money for us to live our sheltered lives in quiet happiness. But then the war came. In September 1939 the Germans marched into Warsaw, and that was the end of our relatively peaceful lives.

By that time, we had two children, a girl of about three and a boy just a few months old. Soon we lived in the ghetto created by the German Gestapo and began to suffer from starvation. The first one of our family to die because of lack of food was the boy. A few days later my husband left our house to look for food as usual but was discovered by a German soldier and killed on the spot by a bullet.

As the war went on, we were not allowed to stay in the Warsaw ghetto any longer. With my little girl I was transported to my first concentration camp, Majdanek [just outside the city of Lublin, approximately 160 kilometers (or 100 miles) southeast of Warsaw], just like Rose Kay [whose story is also in this book] and many others from Warsaw. I was there for only about three weeks when also my little girl died. Now I was all alone. I had lost all I had, all those who made life worth living.

Yet, somehow, my life went on. I went from camp to camp. After Majdanek came Sobibor, Thesbush, Behova, and finally Bergen-Belsen. There I was liberated in April 1945 by the English.

I could have stayed in Behova to be liberated by the Russians. But I thought: "Where am I to go in that big Russia? I have nobody there. I don't know where to go from here. Does it make any difference where I go? I may as well go along with others in the train to Bergen-Belsen." And that is what I did. I was not sure whether it was the right thing to do and I did not care much about it either.[2]

Life in the camps was rough and tough. We all suffered. We did not get enough to eat, often we could not sleep, and we did not have the right clothes. In the winter they gave us summer clothes, and in the summer we got winter clothes; men got women's clothes and women were dressed in men's clothes. We got a tiny little piece of bread to eat and often lots of watery soup. In the meantime we were expected to work hard in the ammunition factories. This went on in most of the camps till, finally, I got sick in Bergen-Belsen. I got typhus, and with it, diarrhea. My weight went down to 40 kilograms [90 pounds].

I just lived on, from one day to the next. Sometimes I thought: "I should pray." And sometimes: "I am going to die." But usually I did not think at all. I was numb, walking in a daze, as if I was heavily drugged. I was there and I was not there. I saw nothing and yet I saw much. I heard nothing and yet I heard a lot. I did not think any more, I did not hope any more, I was like a living corpse. Anything that is bad happened to me. Name it and I got it. I had lost all my dear ones, my husband, my son, and my daughter. I was beaten and starved. I had to work hard. If I could not keep up, they would shoot me. They gave me a bundle of stuff, and I had to walk all day back and forth, back and forth. My life was no life; it was hard work with very little food and very little sleep. When you are hungry, you cannot sleep. When you are cold, you cannot sleep. Yet I knew I could not complain or protest. For if I did this, I would lose even that little piece of bread. So, on I went. At six o'clock they would wake us up for the roll call. The guards had to count us, and they counted us over and over again, up to ten or twenty times. Of course, nobody is missing. Where could we go? And this roll call goes on twice a day. In the winter, it is terrible. But if you would not show up, you are dead. In any case, I often wished that I was dead.

I had male and female guards. They should all be killed, like they killed us. Many of them are now in hiding, but there must be plenty of them yet. They all should be brought to justice.

When the war ended, I was in Bergen-Belsen. English soldiers liberated us. That was the end of our slavery. The English gave us food, they gave us clothes, they gave us a place to live. I worked for them for a short while, till I got married for the second time. I was then 32 years of age and I knew that life had to go on. So when David Bross asked me to marry him, I accepted.

He was also Polish, also a Jew, also a survivor. He was married before the war, but his wife also did not make it. All my husband had left was one cousin. We asked him to come to live with us, but he did not answer. We went from Bergen-Belsen to a former camp, Majdanek.

Our cousin in Canada arranged for our immigration papers, and we could travel as private people, whereas many others had to wait a long time. First we traveled to Holland; from there we took a boat to England, and another boat brought us from England to Halifax in Nova Scotia, Canada. In Halifax we boarded the train, and after a long ride we arrived in Galt, Ontario, and a cousin picked us up. We stayed in his house for about six weeks. Then we found our own home.

My husband was a baker and soon he was working. After about one year we were able, thanks to the generosity of a nice cousin, to rent our own bakery. Soon I helped in the store, though I knew very little English. Even today my English is very poor.

Everything went very well with the bakery and with our new life as well, until 1952, when my second husband died in the seventh year of our marriage. Since that time I am again alone. This is what I have been now for 36 years, a widow. At first I tried to keep the bakery going, but after awhile I sold the business. I said to myself, "This is enough for me."

One bright spot in this somber story is that we have one child, a boy. He did very well. He became a teacher and lives in Toronto. He married a very nice Jewish girl, who became a medical doctor. And she is not just an M.D. but has also a doctorate in pharmacology. And these two have three beautiful children. A son, a daughter-in-law, and three grandchildren—that is all I have.

I started doing some needlepoint work, which I really enjoyed. I also became a volunteer in St. Mary's hospital. Having suffered much, I tried to give some help and perhaps some comfort to other sufferers. And I also like very much to visit my children, and I enjoy especially my three grandchildren. Seeing them, I know I am not alone and my life was not in vain.

Usually my children are coming to my home for *Yom Kippur* and for some other holidays. Then we go together to *shul*. We are having a good time. My grandchildren go to a Jewish school in Toronto. You see, my daughter-in-law is very religious. I am not very orthodox. I go to *shul*, but not every Sabbath. For me it is just a tradition, I am observing, for after all I am still a Jewish person. I eat *kosher* food and keep the Sabbath day. For the rest, I don't know. I wonder who is God? What did He do when I was in the camps? He is supposed to know everything that happens. Why did he not help us? I lost everything. What can I say? During the Second World War six million Jews died and that is not peanuts!

I survived. We, Jews from Poland, did better than the Jews from Holland or from Hungary. None of those survived in our block. They were not tough enough. They were weak people, but we, Polish Jews, were already used to suffering and to a hard life. I could take all they did to me in stride.

Who is God? Where is he? Where was he during World War II? I don't know. I made it. But often I have wished to be dead. In the camp we had no Jewish holidays, no *kosher* food, no Sabbaths, no prayers. All days were the same. We worked hard. We just kept on moving. We had no friends, no relatives. We all lived as long as life lasted, each one for himself or herself.

All we were was a number. When I came to the first work camp in Majdanek, there were still many of us. The Germans did not have time to tattoo a number on our arms; we were just given a piece of wood with a number on it. We were supposed to hang it around our neck with the piece of string attached to it.

Yes, I am happy to live in Canada. I have not been back in Warsaw. I don't want to go there. I have nobody there. Even to build up a new life in Canada was hard. When my second husband died, I was just thirty nine.

Sometimes I still have nightmares. I am standing again in the snow for endless roll calls. My feet are freezing cold. Even telling you my story today will haunt me for a few days. That is why some survivors don't want to be interviewed. They don't want to be reminded of that awful time. They try hard to forget. But they can't. They never will.

Notes

1 Information in this chapter has also been published in "A farewell to a peaceful life: The story of Eva Bross (1913–1989)," *Christian Courier*, May 31, 1999, pp. 18-19.

2 In the last few months of the war, a few groups of prisoners perhaps had an option either to remain at eastern camps about to be "liberated" by the Russians or to be transported to camps in more central areas of Germany. Thousands of Jewish prisoners were moved to Bergen-Belsen from the eastern camps in late 1944.

chapter eight
TOM FAHIDY'S STORY
THE SURVIVAL OF A HUNGARIAN
JEWISH BOY

I. My Survival

My first name is Thomas. I am now a Canadian, but I was born in Hungary, in 1934 (in Hungary my name was Tamás). We lived in Budapest. We were a middle-class family, and as an only child, I received much love and attention from my parents. I dearly loved them both. My father had seven brothers and four sisters; several lived in the capitol. Before World War II we belonged to an Orthodox Jewish congregation, but we were not orthodox in the strict sense of the word.

My recollection of times before 1944 is rather sporadic. I lived a sheltered life and enjoyed elementary school. One of my aunts who was sort of a self-appointed family chronicler told me much later that I was good at mischief. By 1944 I began to realize that times were by no means good and were going to get much worse. I grew up quickly, especially during the last war years, 1944–45.

First my father was taken to a forced labor camp in mid-1944; then my mother was deported with many others not long before Christmas 1944. Jews in Budapest were forced to move into specifically designated apartment buildings to await their fate. The elderly and the very young went to the Budapest ghetto for destruction by the Germans and the Arrow Cross. Those in between were taken away into Germany. My mother miraculously survived the Holocaust in the Belsen-Bergen concentration camp, but she (with many others) caught typhoid fever and died there before she could return to Budapest. A good friend of hers, who was with her in the camp, told my father about this in 1945, when she came back from Sweden where she had recuperated in a Red Cross compound.

[In December 1944,] I was left in this "Jewish house" with two cousins and an elderly relative who was allowed to stay there to look after us. One day she walked out of the place when rumor reached us that our forced move into the ghetto was imminent. The three of us, after tearing the yellow star off our jackets, left shortly afterwards. We walked out amidst heavy artillery fire and went to the building where a distant Gentile relative of one of our cousins lived. I imagine the people in the air-raid shelter where we were all cramped together knew we were Jews but, happily, they did not denounce us.

We were liberated there on January 17, 1945. We left after a few days to find out if there was anybody in the family still alive. I was lucky. I found one of my aunts who came out of hiding, and about a week later I was reunited with my father. My father had run away from his camp in late 1944, got safely behind the front line, and followed the Red Army as it fought its way to Budapest.

One of the saddest memories of my life is that moment when my father found out that my mother had been deported. He broke down and cried. I will never forget the pain in that crying. I then understood how much my father loved my mother.

Most of our family members perished in the Holocaust. But in 1945 we had little time to do much thinking about it. The war had destroyed Budapest almost completely. There was much to do: find food and shelter, start removing the ruins, and rebuild. My first year in secondary school was short. My father remarried in late 1947 (or early 1948). Normality was slowly re-established.

In 1952 I finished high school and began my university studies. I came to Canada in January 1957, after the Hungarian revolution, and finished my studies in Canada and in the United States. After receiving my doctorate, I became a university professor. I have two sons from my first marriage, which ended in divorce. I am now married for the second time. Between my wife and myself, we have six grandchildren. We are affiliated with a Reform Jewish congregation and observe the dietary laws and many other customs of our faith.

I have not only survived, but also have managed to put my life in order. I am grateful to God for both.

II. Hungary's Survival

The Hungarians are related to the Finns and the Estonians and originated from Asia Minor. They settled in the Danube valley. After a number of wars, their prince Géza established peace with the German Emperor Otto the Great at the end of the first millennium.

During the beginning of the second millennium many Hungarians became Christians and associated with the Church of Rome rather than of Byzantium. After the disastrous Mongolian invasion in the 13th century, Hungary became a powerful nation under a number of strong and determined kings. The Turks were driven away and abandoned most of Europe by the end of the 17th century. After that, Hungary was divided into three parts until the time of the Austrian-Hungarian monarchy (1867-1918). In 1916 Emperor Franz-Joseph died and was succeeded by the last king, Charles IV, who abdicated the throne in November 1918. The Monarchy collapsed and Hungary became independent.

In 1919 communist leaders led an uprising of the working class. The dictatorship of the proletariat lasted only a few months. It was replaced by the rule or government of the leader of the counter-revolution, Admiral Miklós Horthy. His new right-wing government was very much opposed to Leninist Communism. Since many Jews were considered to be have been left-wing agitators, about 7000 of them were executed in a cruel slaughter. Anti-Semitism was on the rise, and many Jews emigrated to the New World or tried to do so.

After World War I, the treaty of Trianon gave away a large part of defeated Hungary: Romania, Czechoslovakia, and Yugoslavia were the major recipients of this division. The country was reduced in size to about one-fourth of its former area, and its population was reduced from almost 21 million to 7.5 million. Moreover, this truncated Hungary had to pay a tremendous amount in war debts.

When Hitler came to power in Germany in 1933, the Hungarian government sought closer ties with Germany and with its National Socialism, and later with Italy, hoping to reverse the effect of the treaty of Trianon. Hungary constantly feared Russia and its Communist dictatorship. Thus Hungary sailed a careful course between the Scylla and the Charybdis: it tried to survive with at last some independence between two evil super-powers.

During World War II, Germany generally respected Hungarian territory until 1944. Raw materials and agricultural products that Germany received from Hungary saved it during these years from military occupation. The existing Hungarian government remained in power.

When it became clear that Germany was losing the war, Admiral Horthy asked the Western powers for a truce in October 1944. This was ultimately a futile gesture because the German army had virtually occupied Hungary since early 1944 under pretext of the presence of Soviet forces in Eastern Hungary. Admiral Horthy was put under house arrest, his Government was dissolved, and the Germans put the Hungarian Nazi party, called the Arrow Cross Party, into power.

Beginning March 1944, Jews were obliged to wear the yellow star, and serious prosecution began, culminating in mass deportations. The final outcome of this short-lived but intensive madness was that about 550,000 Jews, more than two-thirds of the total Jewish population, perished. When World War II ended in 1945, Hungary was under Soviet occupation. In 1949 the Soviets established the Hungarian People's Republic, a vassal state of the Soviet Union.

In October 1956 the Hungarian uprising took place, and about 200,000 refugees escaped to other European countries, North America, and Australia. The uprising was put down by the Red Army, and Jánas Kádár was appointed as Chief of State. After awhile, he embarked on a course of tolerance.

In 1989 Hungary returned to democracy and became once again a multi-party state.

III. Where Was God?

Where was God during the war years and the Holocaust especially? How is it possible that God, Who is the source of all morality, could permit so much immorality to take place; how could He allow the death of six million Jews and of millions of Gypsies and other human beings?

My personal feeling is that the question is meaningless from a theological point of view. Who are we to take God to task? We cannot understand God. We cannot answer the question unless we humanize God and ascribe to Him all kinds of human characteristics. But then we have made a God in our likeness, while the Scriptures tell us that it is just then other way around: God made us in His likeness. God is free and sovereign and not human. We cannot put God in the box of our thinking. The only choice we have is that we either believe in God or we don't.

During the war and after the war, many people lost their faith in God, but strangely enough for many others their faith in God became stronger. I have tried to resolve this dilemma for myself. My belief in God became stronger, but I cannot know why He allowed the Holocaust. Instead of asking "why?" I am grateful that I am among the survivors.

One may well ask: how is it possible that a highly civilized people of *Kulturmenschen* could commit such crimes? How could the bullies of the camps come home and sing with their children *"Silent night, holy night"*?

One way to answer this question is to argue that civilization is just a thin veneer on the outside; inside we are still barbarians. There might be some truth in this observation. A Holocaust could happen again, given certain circumstances. In principle, persecution of believers and destructive cruelty as shown in this last Holocaust could happen again at any time and in any place.

This means that we must be on our guard. We should monitor carefully what is happening in the world and be sensitive to the rise of evil forces from time to time. We can never forget what happened. It has left us with an aching void. We know now what hatred can do. Hatred is able to destroy humanity. We must fight hatred. And this fight may well be a never-ending one. This is perhaps the most important lesson we learned from the Holocaust.

chapter nine
JOHN & MANIA KAY'S STORY

We listened first to John's story, then to Mania's story.

My Jewish name is Moshe Jacob Kujowski, but I changed it to John Kay after I came to Canada because my Jewish name is Polish and difficult to spell.

I was born in Krosniewice, Poland, on July 25, 1906. I became a tailor. In Poland most Jewish people learned a trade, and we lived close together in a city like Krosniewice. We were not living in a ghetto. For the first 33 years of my life I was a free man. Yet life was not always easy. Poland was a poor country and the Polish people liked to stir up trouble. Whenever they did, Jews became the targeted victims.

In 1939 the Germans invaded Poland and our city was bombed heavily. I ran away for safety's sake and lived in a farmer's orchard for two or three weeks. But in the end I had to return to the city. I was married and had two children. Before the occupation I had been politically active, so I soon became suspect. It must have been for this reason that we were thrown out of our house. We had to find other places to live. This was not easy. We moved from one address to another. After three moves, we were not allowed to find our own accommodation, but were assigned to the ghetto. That happened in 1940.

We were still together as a family but had to live in localities that looked like stables. Living conditions were terrible and hard to describe. But even living in the ghetto did not last long.

WHERE WAS GOD?

[Ed. note: John lost his wife and children and worked and lived in different concentration camps during the war, but he did not tell us much about this time. His story continues in 1945.]

I was released from the concentration camp on April 29th. But I still was not free. I lived in a train for about three weeks. But the train had no place to go; it moved back and forth. Finally we arrived at Auschwitz [about 55 kilometers (35 miles) west of Krakow in southern Poland]. However, we could not stay there either and we were transported to Buchenwald [in east-central Germany, near Weimar]. But there the Americans came closer all the time. So the Germans put us back on the train and again we moved back and forth. At several locations the rails had been hit by bombs and we had to return. Finally we came to an area where the rails were not damaged. There were men going to work who would throw food to us on the train. But the soldiers did not tolerate this. They threatened to shoot them.

This train brought us to Dachau [in southern Germany, near München]. But the train was bombed before we got there. I was one of the six out of the seventy-two in our car who survived. When after twenty-one days they opened the doors of the railroad car, the six of us who were still alive were commanded to come out. I fell out of the train. The fresh air made me dizzy and deadly tired. A German soldier asked me whether I would like to lie down there on the ground to die or would want to move on. So I got up and went into the camp. Only two days later the Americans came in and brought us some food.

I was free now, and after I had recovered somewhat, I went to Bergen-Belsen [in northwestern Germany] to look for my wife and children. They had not survived. But there I found Mania and a year later, in 1946, we were married. For a while we lived in München.

I remember how we once went to the opera. We looked around in that auditorium. Now we were supposed to be the winners and the Germans the losers. But it was just the other way around. We had hardly any clothes to wear, but they came dressed quite elegantly. Mania was walking in shoes two sizes too small for her. We had nothing. So we wondered who were the winners and who the losers?

In München our oldest daughter was born. In 1948 we were able to immigrate to Canada. There we had our second daughter.

Mania's story:

I was born in Auschwitz [the village of Oswiecim, in southern Poland] on December 1, 1920. My Hebrew name is Mirjam. My last name at that time was Bodner. I was 19 when the Germans came. Then things began to change quickly. In 1940 the ghetto was built and we were compelled to live inside that specific area of the city. Living conditions in the ghetto were disgusting. Three families had to share one room. There were no washrooms and no facilities to cook a meal. We could not wash ourselves properly. Every day I had to march out of the ghetto with many others to a factory run by the Germans. We had to work 12 to 14 hours and received no pay and only very little food. We were always hungry. From one day to the next, we were not sure that we could make it home. The Germans were always rounding up people who could not make it any longer and sending them to the gas chambers. I was married already and came home in the evening to my husband in our crowded room.

Then in August 1943 the ghetto was completely liquidated. There had been many liquidations before. Many had been killed already. In this final liquidation so many people were murdered that their dead bodies, covered with blood and mud, were piled up high in the streets. Since it was very hot that August, flies covered the decomposing bodies.

Those who had not been killed had to walk a few kilometers to the nearest train station. I walked with my sister and her two children. Our parents and husbands had been killed already. I noticed that the lips of my niece were dried out and cracking. We stopped briefly and I tried to find some water for her. But an SS-guard ran up to me with a pistol in each hand, shouting that he would gun her down if I got any water for her. So on we went. All I could do was to spit on a hankie and wet her lips with my saliva. All during this walk we had to be very careful. The guards had fierce German shepherds, trained to attack people and rip them to shreds.

We were loaded on cattle trains: babies, old people, sick people, young people, children. We were squeezed in like sardines in a tin. Buckets had to serve as toilets. The smell was awful. There was no room to change, no privacy whatsoever.

In the end we arrived at Auschwitz. The doors of the train were opened. We could get out. There was much shouting and many were beaten. The guard dogs attacked us. Children, older people, and dead bodies were just thrown out of the train.

As we stood there outside, they tried to segregate us. I had already lost my husband and parents, so I wanted to stay with my sister and her two children. I told this to the SS-guard who was watching us. He responded by kicking me in the face. I lost several teeth. Then he said, "If your sister abandons those kids and goes to work, you can stay together." Naturally my sister refused to do this. But I was still young and strong. For me the only thing to do was to go to work. Thus I lost at that moment the last ones of my family. From then on I was all by myself, alone.

We were escorted from the train station to the main camp. There we were taken into a sauna. We had to strip down. Our heads were shaved. We had a bath but it was torture. Guard dogs would jump on us. Guards would whip us for nothing. We were tattooed on the forearm while we were in the sauna. Here is my number: 52889. Because the tattooing hurt, I made a face; thus I was beaten severely. Then striped prison clothes that would not fit were given to me. Off we went to the barracks.

I had come to Auschwitz with family and friends. But I walked out of the sauna a different being, an anonymous thing. I did not know anymore who I was or what I was. I simply was 52889.

First I was sent to what was called a quarantine camp. There I could see the smoke of the crematoriums, which were only a short distance away from where we lived. I could smell the burning flesh. I knew for sure that there was no hope for the rest of my family. The only family relation

I had in that quarantine camp was a sister-in-law. Once she told me that she had seen my husband working somewhere. But I never saw him again. I never heard from him either. Later I found out that he had been killed in a cruel way. It had been his job to carry a big kettle of coffee to his barracks at breakfast time. Another prisoner stole some coffee from that kettle. Because my husband had not killed the other prisoner, he was guilty and had to be punished. They broke his shoulder joints and hanged him backwards on his hands. A kind of crucifixion. So he died a painful death. Others—my parents, my sister and her children—all went straight away to the crematorium.

I am not sure how long I stayed in quarantine. We could not leave our barracks. Nobody was allowed to go to the washroom until the whole group could go. The situation in our barracks was atrocious. There were rats, worms, and lice all over the place. It was dirty. There was no water to clean oneself. At night we were often cold, having nothing to cover ourselves. During the summer we often burned from the heat. Twice each day we stood outside to be counted as if we were very precious. Often we stood in the snow for hours on end.

At nightfall the guards would come to round up people for the crematorium. They would blow their whistles and yell *"Blocksperre, Blocksperre!"* and would collect the ones to be burned that night. They were lined up outside. No one of us inside was allowed to look out of the window. At one time we had a number of Greeks in our barracks. They had prayed and fasted all day long, but still that night, they too were taken to the crematorium. This happened also with the gypsies. We had been jealous of them because they had stayed together as families. But now we saw how they were terminated as undesirable individuals.

In our barracks, I became very sick with typhoid. I did not expect to survive. My sister-in-law, who was close by in another barracks, managed to help me. Every evening she brought me clean water to drink. To do this she had to pass through a gate guarded by an SS-man. She could easily have been killed for what she was doing. Once she even managed to take me along to her own barracks. The oldest woman there was in charge and thus responsible for all prisoners in that barrack. She looked at me and said: "This one will not make it through the night." Yet, somehow, I did survive. And slowly I became a bit stronger again.

There is one awful thing I remember from that time. The Germans take pride in being a clean people. I still smell the chlorine which was everywhere present. Often they were more interested in cleaning buildings than in helping people to keep clean. But one time they wanted to do both. We all had to leave the barracks, and the guards threw everything out. It was a very cold day. We were told to assemble in the middle of the yard where there was a big pot full of an antiseptic solution. We were commanded to undress in order to get rid of all the lice. Our rags were thrown into a pit to be burned. There we stood, naked, a few hundred women. We had to take a bath in the big pot with the solution. This burned like fire, since our bodies had many sores from the lice. Many of us were crying. Meanwhile, a number of German SS-men and women laughed, made fun, and took pictures. Never before had I felt so low and so humiliated. Praying, I asked, "God, if you are there, please open the ground so that they all can sink down and be buried alive." Having been brought up in a strict home, I felt terrible standing there naked and being laughed at. Why should I keep on living? It was not worth the trouble. There was no dignity left. I just wanted to die.

At another time, also in 1943, I stood in the snow without shoes. My sister-in-law brought me one wooden shoe. We were standing in the roll call line to be counted. I kept shifting the wooden shoe from one foot to the other, afraid that the SS-guards would discover that I still had one shoe. I thought: "This is it. Here I am. A number, nothing more. Naked and barefoot. It cannot get worse. I see no way out." Again I asked myself: "Why should I go on living?" I hoped I could lie down somewhere to die. Life was just hell.

Around that time, they started to look for people still able to work. An SS-guard, who happened to be the head of the working commission, came to our quarantine barracks with a heavy, carved leg of a dining-room table on his shoulder. He selected people for work by hitting them with that leg. I was hit across the lower back. Happily I was not injured too badly. Often I feared that I would be crippled from being hit so badly that I would have to go to the hospital. I knew that those who were sent to the hospital did not return. I always tried to stay out of reach of the SS-guards. Yet sometimes I did not avoid them and I was hit several times. Most likely the result of such cruel treatment was that one of my kidneys had to be removed after I came to Canada.

However, in 1943, having been selected to work, I was moved to another part of the camp. Every morning we went by truck through the city to the factory where they dropped us off for work.

But in May 1944 things changed. Hungarian people were brought in, and the food rations increased because of this. We did not understand why, but we were happy nevertheless.

But this did not last. From the main camp we were moved to a smaller one. I worked now in another factory. I stood in an assembly line and had to cut wires or make screws. It was hard labor. I knew that what we made was used for the war. All the time we were under guard by SS-ers with their bloodthirsty dogs.

In January 1945 it became clear that the Germans were losing the war. The Russians were approaching. We heard their guns. They were close by. If only the Germans had left us where we were, we would soon have been liberated and freed. But somehow they wanted to keep us. On January 18, they tried to liquidate Auschwitz and the surrounding camps. We were rounded up like cattle. We stood in the assembly line for a long time and, finally, we marched from our small camp through the town to join the people from the Buna camp.[1] Then we had to walk about 40 kilometers [25 miles] to get from Auschwitz to Gleiwitz.[2] But it was January and very cold. We were not dressed for the outdoors. We also became very hungry. We had not been allowed to take any food with us. People who gave up and fell down were shot to death. After awhile, I felt I could not breathe anymore. I begged my friends to leave me there. I could not make it. I was ready to die. But my friends dragged me along, one on each side. That is how I made it.

In Gleiwitz we were loaded once again on cattle trains. Our box car had an open roof. I don't know what happened to me in that train. In the freezing cold, we huddled together as closely as possible to keep warm. My friends tell me that I was unconscious. People would step on me, but I would not notice it. The train moved back and forth for a long time. It had no place to go to. The Russians were everywhere already. Finally we stopped at another work camp, but it had no space left.

So on we went until we finally arrived in Bergen-Belsen [a trip of more than 500 kilometers (300 miles), to northern Germany]. There we were unloaded. Yet many had died during the transport. There was not enough space to dispose of the bodies. So they were piled up along the tracks. Every day trains came with more prisoners. But the situation was desperate. There was no work, no food, no water. People were dying like flies. Such were the last days of the war.

Finally, on April 15, 1945, the English troops arrived and marched into the camp. I had just enough strength to stand at the gate. The soldiers could not believe what they saw. They were beside themselves. People were dying everywhere. Corpses were lying all around. None of us had the strength to dig a grave. The dead bodies were covered with flies. It was hard to see so many die while freedom was just around the corner. The English soldiers tried to help us. They gave us food. But actually this was a mistake. We had not eaten for two weeks and we had no water. Of the low number of survivors many got sick with diarrhea. Some of them died. They died from eating good food. It was just too much. Their stomachs could not stand normal food. We survivors were, in fact, just corpses barely alive. We needed medical help badly, but it took awhile for the medics to come. The war was not over yet, and they were needed elsewhere.

Here I met John. After some time, I went back to Auschwitz rather than to my home town. I wanted to see the ghetto once more. There I had some business to take care of. In the ghetto we had at one time built a hiding place or a bunker. I remember how, while we were living in the ghetto, we once had been tipped off that the SS-ers were coming. We hid our parents in a shack and threw all kinds of things on top of them to protect them and help them survive. It worked; the guards did not find them.

Such was life in the ghetto. You were never safe and never sure. You never knew what the next day would bring, not even the next hour. There was a never-ending anxiety, fear and worry. The struggle for life was a thing beyond description. It killed many. How I had the strength to make it through all this, I still don't understand.

In the ghetto I found my possessions in the hiding place where I had left them. But by now all of it was moldy. Yet I took it out. Some of it was still usable.

John came also to Auschwitz. During the beginning of the war, he and his brother had worked for the commandant as a tailor. After the war, he joined the Intelligence Service for two weeks. He was involved in capturing the chief of the so-called "Laboratory of Experiment." This man was to be brought to justice for war crimes.

We continued the interview with some questions.

Why was it that you, Polish people, have a larger number of survivors than others?

JOHN: Most of my professional friends did not survive. Most Dutch people did not survive. Greek people did not either. But we did.

MANIA: Some beautiful women from France came to the camp, but they could not survive. I think that we, Polish people, survived because we were used to a hard life. Yet before the war, Polish peasants usually were worse off than we, Jews. That is why at times they tried to destroy us.

Where did the two of you meet each other?

MANIA: We met in Bergen-Belsen. John was looking there for family. We got to know each other and after one year we married. We moved to Münich and lived there till we emigrated to Canada in 1948. Our first daughter was born in Münich, the second one in Canada.

Also in Canada we faced a lot of hardships. Canada was not ready for the big-scale immigration of the late '40s. We came with a 14-month-old daughter. Most people did not want to rent us a place to live. They did not trust us. And we could not communicate. You can hear people and see people, but you cannot talk to them. They don't understand you. It's awful.

JOHN: After coming to Canada I worked for two months in a tailor shop and then I started my own business in Kitchener. I thought I knew enough English by then.

While you were in those concentration camps, was there still an opportunity for worship services or at least for prayer?

JOHN: Usually there was no place to pray. There was no Sabbath. At Easter, Yom Kippur, and Hanukkah, selections were made: people went off to the gas chambers. Thus we knew that it was the time of one of our holidays.

MANIA: Yes, they knew the dates of our holidays. Most of the killings happened at that time. We were worse off than animals. I envied the guard dogs. Those German shepherds were treated with more love and respect than we. I often prayed for the privilege of dying, since I felt that I did not have the strength to survive.

Before the war, did you regularly attend the synagogue?

JOHN: I was not a regular attendant. I was a modern man. But now I observe the Jewish Sabbath and go regularly to the synagogue.

MANIA: I was born and raised in a strictly Orthodox Jewish home. I even took private lessons to learn Hebrew. I still am not fluent in it. Yet I can pray in Hebrew. I am fluent in Yiddish. I speak Yiddish, German, and Polish.

Do you think Judaism will survive?

MANIA: The Jewish religion has survived for thousands of years. I am sure it will survive. The Jews have suffered so much just because they are Jews. I am a strong believer in Judaism. I am also a Zionist. I was brought up as a Zionist. I believe in Judaism and Zionism. I have been to Israel. I love Israel. The state of Israel simply is a miracle.

Do you still believe that you are God's chosen people, the elect?

JOHN: I don't like to say that we are special. I like us to be just like everybody else.

MANIA: But yet we are a special people. I don't know why we were persecuted because of being Jewish. Being Jewish is no crime, but persecution goes far back in history. Is it because we are intelligent or smart or something?

Often circumstances lead to hate. This was the case in Poland. The peasants lived in miserable conditions. They lived like poor slaves. They worked for the land-owners and had to pay them money for the land. They were often starving. Then the priest would come and say to them: "Look at those Jews. See how well they live." And in this way the church promoted hating the Jews, what is called anti-Semitism.

Were there any changes in your faith during or since the war? Was there a change in your views on religion, the Torah, or God's guidance and providence?

MANIA: I come from a very observant, strict Jewish home. But in the concentration camps I had my doubts about God when I was standing in the roll-call lines and was seeing the smoke rising from the chimneys, smelling the stench of burning flesh. I asked myself: "Is there a God? Really? If so, why doesn't He do something?"

After the liberation when I married again and started a new family, I returned to my faith. I saw that God was still with us. In spite of all our losses, it was a miracle that now we could look forward again and start a new chapter in our life-story. Even in my dreams I had never expected to have a family again. In the camps all I had dreamt about was of not being hungry anymore and being able to eat all the bread I wanted. We dreamt always about food.

But God has been good to me. I believe again. I really do.

What about the German people? Can you stand meeting them and hearing them talk?

MANIA: Once a German came into our store and told us that there had never been a Holocaust. It was not true what we were saying. I became very upset at that time. I told him to leave the store. But he was an exception. Most German people try not to talk about it. But I never hid my number. They could see that: this is proof enough.

Were the numbers always on the lower arm?

JOHN: Up to the end of 1942 that is where the numbers were. But in 1943 people got it on their chest. I have under my number half a star, a sign that I am a Jew.

Should the war criminals be brought to justice or should we just forgive them?

MANIA: I think they should be punished even if they are in their 80s. My mother does not live any more. She was killed while she was still a young, beautiful woman. Why should war criminals, even if they are old men by now, have the right to live when my mother was killed at such a young age? Justice should be done. War criminals should pay for their crimes. They are responsible for what they did, no matter how old they are now. It was so easy for them to kill. They killed at a moment's notice. There was nobody to protest and protect the innocent victims. It seemed that the whole world was asleep.

Even after the war we continued to suffer. We lived in Münich for some time. In Europe we were "DPs," displaced persons. There were not many friendly countries we could go to. I did not want to stay in Europe. Europe was a graveyard. There the earth was too red with blood. So we came to Canada. But immigration is a hard thing too. You come to a strange country, you have no friends, you don't understand the language. It has taken me a lifetime to adapt. But, yes, there are also many very nice people too. One lady named Janzen gave us a break. She lent us a place where we could open a store free of rent. This helped us a great deal. It was a nice breakthrough in lots of misery.

Did you meet more helpful people? Were there any Christian friends?
MANIA: Not all people who say they serve God are nice people. Most German people believe in God. And yet they did what even the devil would not do.[3] And many of them still claim that it did not happen. The concentration camp in Dachau[4] was in the middle of the city. Did they not see the smoke rising from the ovens? Did they not smell the stench of burning flesh? They saw the prisoners walking in rags. What did they do with the clothes they took from us?

Poland was the worst country. You can count on your fingers the number of Poles who helped us Jews. Yet we grew up with them as children. We played together. We lived together as neighbors. But when the Germans came and took over, the Poles changed faces. They did not know us anymore. They dressed up in German uniforms. They thought they were mighty rulers now. We could not talk to them anymore. They sold us for as little as a few cups of sugar.

Has your life become more peaceful now?
MANIA: In general it has. But I still have bad dreams. I dream of being chased. Sometimes my husband gets up in the morning saying "I was in the camp last night."

What has happened stays with you all the time.

[*Ed. note:* John died in 1991. Mania moved to her new
apartment and through the 1990s visited schools, telling
a new generation about the Holocaust.]

Notes
1 The Buna camp is also mentioned in the story of Jack and Miriam Somer.
2 Gleiwitz, also mentioned in the story of Jack and Miriam Somer, is about

40 kilometers [25 miles] northwest of Auschwitz. Many have wondered why the Nazis kept moving Jewish and other prisoners even in the last weeks of the war. Likely the Nazis continued using those "slave" laborers to help construct a few defensive fortifications back in Germany in late 1944. The Nazis, perhaps feeling guilty about their evil camps, tried to remove at least some of the "evidence" of their atrocities. That they kept operating the camps into the last few weeks of the war indicates their obsession to kill as many prisoners as possible.

3 Isaiah 29:13 (NIV): "The Lord says: 'These people come to me with their mouth and honor me with their lips, but their hearts are far from me.'" This verse is later quoted by Jesus; see Matthew 15:8.

4 Dachau Concentration Camp, near Münich in southern Germany, was established in 1933 and operated until 1945. With its many subcamps, Dachau was a "model" for the Nazi concentration camps system.

chapter ten
ROSE KAY'S STORY

My maiden name is Rosia Rosensweig and I was born on May 5, 1920, in Alexandra Towat Loeki, in Poland. In 1938 as a young bride, I married Soulmendol Isvalewies. My father, who was a very good and caring man, wanted us to get married mainly for safety reasons, especially for my protection.

In 1939 the war began. The Germans invaded Poland. We left Alexandra Towat Loeki and went to Warsaw. Like so many other Jews, we thought it would be safer to live in a large city among many of our fellow Jews. For the first two years of the war, we were quite free and did well in our trades and stores. My husband was a butcher and I worked as a dressmaker in a tailor shop. During that time we were prosperous and enjoyed the big city as well as its large Jewish community.

Then after those two good years, the ghetto was formed. Even in the ghetto we at first had quite a nice home. Since we were not poor, we could relish a number of luxuries many others did not have. We shared what we had gladly with those who were less fortunate. We had no children of our own, which also made it easier for us to help others.

But slowly our situation worsened. My husband lost his job. We were summoned to attend so-called liquidations or selections. When there was a selection, some had to go the left, others to the right. The weak and disabled ones, who had lost their economic value for the German war industry, were summoned to the left and marched off. We never saw or heard from them again. The ones on the right could stay and were put to work.

At that time I was still young and strong. I did not fear the liquidations, but there were many others who did. There were mothers who tried to hide their children in their backpacks. Often these children were discovered. When the German soldiers found these children, they stomped them on their little heads. Poor kids.

The situation in Warsaw deteriorated continually. People were lying on the streets, begging for a piece of bread. I still hear them pleading, begging: "Please, give me a piece of bread. Please, I want to live." It was terrible. And Jews were not the only ones suffering.

Some of us tried to escape the always-threatening presence of German soldiers and SS-men by building hiding places. We had a very nice one that provided shelter, food, and a measure of safety for my sister, her two children, my husband, and myself. But one day, during a liquidation, we were discovered. My husband and I were separated after having been married for only three years. I don't know what happened to him. I never saw him again, but I was told that he died in Warsaw's ghetto.

A little later I was sent off to my first camp, Majdanek [near Lublin in southeast Poland]. Being in my early twenties, I was strong and could stand slave labor. I had a very hard time in the work camp, but I survived.

From Majdanek many other prisoners and I were sent to Auschwitz. There I lost my name and became a number. My number was 46834. I worked again as a dressmaker. At one time I hurt my index finger very badly. I could not work for a while, but my supervisor protected me very nicely. Once again I escaped the storm of racial hate.

My finger healed and I was able to continue with my job. Always I tried to do more than was required. If a volunteer was needed, I was always there. I always tried to work hard and to help my friends. Some of them survived the camp, and I am thankful that they made it because of my help. I am proud of what I was able to do for them.

I remember well how they treated us in Auschwitz. Our heads were shaven and they also shaved us under the arms. Every time this was done, SS-men would look at us women and smile. It was always embarrassing.

As the war came to an end and we could hear the Russian guns nearby, many of us were sent to the crematorium. But others, including myself, were put on a train to be transported to Bergen-Belsen [in northwest Germany]. The Germans did not want us to be in Auschwitz when the Russians would take over. They tried to erase all traces of their cruelties. In that train we had to stand in open cattle cars, 100–150 people per car. Many people died. As we got tired, we sat on the corpses of those who did not make it. They died before freedom came. Their dead bodies looked to us like a comfortable seat after we had been standing endlessly. We were so tired. We were waiting for others to die so that we could sit. It was terrible. The "journey" took a day and a night. Finally, we arrived, exhausted and hungry.

After a few days in Bergen-Belsen, we were liberated by the English army. I remember that I was working with some of my friends in the kitchen preparing some kind of meal when an announcement on the intercom told us that the war was over and that we were free. At first I could not believe that it was really true. I did not know where the voice came from. It was a voice completely different from the barking commands we used to hear. In my confusion and ignorance, I thought the wires themselves were speaking!

After the war, we remained in the camp for some time. We tried to find out whether we still had any relatives and how we could reach them. Not only had my husband died in the Warsaw ghetto, but I found out that so also had my father and mother. I wondered where my brother and sisters were. I could not find them. In Belgen-Belsen, the allied soldiers gave us lists with names of survivors, but my brother and sisters were not on those lists. Apparently, I was now "alone in the world," a stranger for all. Later I sent out letters all over the world. This effort was not entirely without success. Fifteen years later, I found a cousin; but that was all.

In 1947 I married for the second time. Soon afterward, we left for Montreal in Canada. A tailoring company from Montreal had come to Bergen-Belsen to attract new employees. I was among the first ones to be chosen. My new husband was also a tailor. When we arrived in Montreal, the Jewish community there gave us two blankets and found us a room to

stay. The lady who opened her house for us and—as she used to say—
"adopted" us was very nice.

Ten years older than I, my husband was already 37 when we were
married. He was a good tailor and a good husband. He wanted very much
to have a son, but I had difficulty with childbirth. Soon after becoming
pregnant, I would lose the fetus by miscarriage. So in Montreal I decided
not to go back to work but to stay home. Soon I found myself pregnant
again. This time I stayed in bed for the entire nine months. Then our wish
came through; we had a son. My husband had had two sons before the
war from his first marriage, but they both were killed during the Holocaust. He was longing for offspring, and I very much wanted to give him
a child. Our son did well. He grew up, became a lawyer, married a Jewish
girl, and they have two children. This was a rich fulfillment for my husband; it made him very happy.

After we had been in Montreal for two-and-a-half years, we went to
Kitchener to open our own shop. Mr. Jack Somer [whose story also appears in this book] had convinced my husband to take this step. I did not
like it at the time. I cried like a baby. I loved Montreal. It was such a large,
civilized city compared with Kitchener. From the first day of our arrival
in Kitchener, I worked in the tailor shop of John and Mania Kay.

My husband died in 1977 at the age of 67 and I have been again a
widow since. But I am happy with my children and grandchildren. Life is
still good for me. God is good to me. But first it was very hard to lose my
husband again. I often said, "God, why did this have to happen to me?"
My husband was such a hard worker and he was just planning to retire in
1978. Now I was alone again. The house was empty. I often asked myself,
"For whom do I have to cook today?"

You asked me whether I am an observing Jew. The answer is "Yes and
No." I buy my kosher meat. But every so often I go to the steak house for
a nice dinner. And, yes, I go to the synagogue every Sabbath. I have discovered that one cannot live without faith. We are not animals. Here in
Kitchener I used to be a client of a Jewish shoemaker who got married in
a Christian church, but only because his wife wanted this. After his mar-

riage he never saw the inside of the church again, nor the synagogue. Once I asked him why he did not believe in God any more. I told him that I believed in God. I still believe that God is good. I said to him that after the war we were not all dead; there were survivors and we were among them. But to him all this did not mean anything. He just could not believe in God's goodness; he had lost his faith completely.

But sometimes I myself wonder too. It seems hard to keep on believing, especially when I think back on the concentration camps. I cannot tell much about that time. I try to forget all those terrible things. I simply don't like to talk about them.

But often at night in my sleep I cry and holler. I see them coming to me, the soldiers, the SS-men. They come to take me along to some camp, but I refuse. I shout in my sleep: "I have already been there long enough. Why do I have to go to this hell again?"

Yes, life in a concentration camp was very hard. Many died. Yet some of our supervisors were humane and friendly. One of them often was able to persuade the SS-man watching us to go on an errand. Then she told us to sit down and rest. This lady had compassion. If there had not been some like her in the camps, none of us would be here today.

After we had been liberated, I spent about two months in a hospital. I had been under too much stress and my heart was beating too fast. After I recovered, I was asked whether I would like to return to my homeland, Poland. But I was not interested in going there. Why should I go to Poland? I had no one to go home to. I preferred to move to Canada rather than Israel, but soon I discovered that even here life as a Polish immigrant is far from easy.

Later I visited Israel for five weeks. My son made sure that I saw all that I wanted to see. I was surprised. The people in Israel are happy now. They are not hungry or poor anymore. They all make a good living. They might still be the chosen people. But don't ask me anything more. I do not know the answers. Long ago there were times that it seemed they were the chosen ones, but now we have been murdered, six million of us, in the Holocaust. It is not clear what we are. Perhaps in the future our children or grandchildren can look again like the chosen nation. Who knows?

Let me say a final word about the war criminals. There are still quite a few of them alive, but they are old now. It does not make much sense to kill them. It seems to me that it would be much better to direct our attention to the younger generation so that they may learn never to do the things that we have experienced. For me it is good enough to know that Hitler is dead. I only hope that our children and grandchildren never have to suffer as much as we did during the years of the Holocaust.

chapter eleven

ROTA HERZBERG LISTER'S HOLOCAUST EXPERIENCE

"If they take our house,
Goods, fame, child, or spouse ..."

– translated from Martin Luther's
Ein Feste Burg ist Unser Gott, (circa 1530).[1]

The saying that those who do not know their history are bound to repeat it has been shown true repeatedly during the two thousand years of persecution of the Jews. How during all those centuries did Jewish families teach their children about the sufferings they inherited and were likely to experience for themselves? How did they try to escape their horribly predictable fate? I hope that my story will shed some light upon the perplexing questions of persecution, resistance, and survival.

I, too, am a survivor. I did not suffer in a concentration camp, but I suffered from anti-Semitism. I suffered as a Jew in many ways as did many of my relatives. My good uncle Leo, who lost one of his legs in the war of 1914-1918, together with my aunt Emmi and younger cousin Inge were transported to Terezin (Theresienstadt)[2] from their fine apartment house in Cologne. From there they were brought to Auschwitz to be gassed. My cousin Rolf, their son, was able to emigrate to England before 1939 with his fiancee Ilse. I hope he was able to reclaim the property stolen from his murdered parents.

This then is the story of the destruction of my own immediate family. My Jewish father, Karl, was destroyed by a rival's treachery and the Gestapo's harassment. My Protestant mother, Johanna, was made to suffer the loss of all she cherished and the isolation from neighbors and former friends. And I myself, brought up as a Protestant but branded "Jew" from 1933, when I was five year old, by children who only the day before had been my friends and playmates, never had a normal childhood and gradually lost everything of value.

Why should I, too, tell my story? I tell it because a mixed marriage in National Socialist Germany produced its own specific tensions and difficulties. I, the only child of such a mixed marriage, had an uncertain identity and no peers who understood the pressures of one who worshipped as a Christian but suffered as a Jew.

I tell my story because every individual has a story which, however much it may resemble that of others, produces its own spiritual and emotional qualities. It is my duty to share my story with you. I must tell of the goodness of my particular Jewish father, the loyalty of my particular Protestant mother, and the childhood torment and lifelong aftereffects on myself.

Why did all this happen? Why did the world-wide depression of the 1930s produce no other regimes elsewhere like that of the *Reich* of Germany lasting 1933–1945? Why, despite alliances with Hitler and his regime, did fascist Italy and Spain not reach the same level of systematic persecution, dispossession, and destruction of minorities as Nazi Germany? Many have tried to answer this persistent question. For the time being, I leave it to historians.

I came into this world in 1928, just at the threshold of the great depression, which hit Germany deeply. I was born in Iserlohn, in southern Westphalia, formerly a province of Prussia in what is now northwestern Germany. My father, Karl Herzberg, was a Jew. Like many other Jews at that time, he tried to leave behind his Jewish identity and to assimilate completely into German culture. My parents called me Rotraud, an old German name celebrated in the songs of the German romantic Eduard Morike. My beginning could not have been more German than that.

My father was a decorated veteran of World War I. Restless after the end of the war in 1918, he soon went to Italy, where he stayed for three years, trying to make a living in a variety of occupations. He returned to Germany because Italy at that time was too dirty for his liking. He went to Iserlohn, where his uncle owned and operated a needle factory. This uncle offered him a job as a manager in the factory. But this did not last. I am not quite sure exactly what happened. I believe that in those economically hard times the factory was sold. My father was then on his own. He had an office at home and was marketing drapery and other textile products of several firms located in Chemnitz and elsewhere in eastern Germany.

In my great-uncle's factory my father met Johanna Reuter, a German Protestant. They fell in love and married in 1927. The next year I was born. I was to remain their only child. I think that my mother had a miscarriage three years later. It is also quite possible that she induced an abortion herself. Nazism and anti-Semitism were on the rise and frightening. What really happened was never discussed in our home. I remember that my father often took me out for a walk on Sundays. How I loved those walks with "Pappi!" He held my hand and we walked through the outskirts and parks of Iserlohn in southern Westphalia. One Sunday when we came back, my usually industrious mother was in bed. Father told me the typical story of that time: "The stork has bitten Mamma in her leg." I wondered: why would the stork bite Mummy? I thought the stork was a nice bird that brought us babies. Why did he not bring me a baby brother or sister?

The first five years of my life were normal. I grew up like any other German girl. At the age of three I was playing in the sandbox behind our apartment house, Weingarten 7, and I wished fervently that I had a playmate. If this could not be a brother or sister, then perhaps some other little friends would do.

"Mummy," I said, "I want to have children too!" Apparently my parents understood my need for companionship. They enrolled me in a fine private nursery school called *Kindergarten*. *Tante* (Aunt) Hannah, our supervisor and teacher, was nice and had thick, shiny braids wound around her head. She was a lot nicer than Herta, my *Kindermaedchen* (nurse-maid). In *Tante* Hannah's *Kindergarten*, I could play with many girls and boys. When a photograph was taken, I, the youngest in the class, was sitting on *Tante* Hanna's lap. I liked all the other children, but especially Roland, who was my boyfriend. But he often got us into trouble, and then both of us had to stand in separate corners of the classroom because we had been "naughty."

In the winter 1931–1932 I was almost four years old. I had been selected to recite a Christmas poem in front of all the parents and the other children. My Mummy helped me to memorize the beautiful lines about a winter encounter with the Christchild: *"Denkt Euch, Ich habe das Christkind geseh'n"* (Imagine, I have seen the Christchild). My Mummy would have become an excellent teacher if her parents could have afforded to send her to a teachers' college. But because *Opa* (Grandpa), who lost one of his legs in the war of 1914-1918, was just a factory foreman, Mummy had to go to work after grade 8. Yet she did many artistic things, like tie-dying. She also made me a beautiful winter hat with embroidered flowers. My Mummy was such a nice person.

Next Christmas was even better. Roland played Joseph and I was Mary, acting and singing in the Christmas play for all the parents and children in attendance. In January 1933 I turned five, eager to go to a real school in one more year and learn to read and write. I enjoyed looking at my beloved picture books and could read some words already.

Daddy told us that there would be a new government. He did not like what he heard and saw. He said, "If Hitler comes to power, there will be another war." Daddy did not like war. He was only 21 years old when the war of 1914 broke out and he was drafted. He suffered from the cold on the Eastern front in Russia and his jaw became badly infected.

Then in 1933 everything changed. *"Jude, Jude,"* the other Kindergarten children screamed at me. I didn't know what that meant, but I knew that they weren't friendly the way they used to be. I ran home in tears because they were mean to me, and I asked my parents what was meant by

"*Jude, Jude.*" It was news to me. I had not been aware of my being partly Jewish. It seemed that being a Jew was wrong. My parents looked at each other with anxious eyes and then explained to me in what sense I was different from the other children. My father was a Jew by birth, though not in religious practice. They told me that cousin Rolf would soon have his Bar Mizvah in a Synagogue. I had never been in one because my Daddy did not go there, and Mummy did not go to her Protestant church any more either. I didn't really understand much of what they tried to explain to me. But I learned soon enough that the other children didn't want to play with me any more.

My parents decided that Iserlohn was too small for a family with a Jew as the head of the household. So we moved to a much larger industrial city, Dortmund in the Ruhr district in west central Germany, where we would not be so well known. We found an attractive home in the suburb Dortmund-Brackel, occupying the ground floor in a three-story house owned by a widow, who lived on the second floor with her divorced daughter and a grandson, Guenter. The attic floor was occupied by a working-class family with a son, Helmut, about ten or eleven years old. So this was the situation: three families in one house, each with one child. We lived there till after the terrible *Kristallnacht* of November 9/10, 1938.

In 1934, the three of us children all went to the same school. Guenter and I were in the first year and Helmut was in a class for older children. At first, things went well with me. I played with the neighborhood children. Mummy wanted me to be perfectly behaved at all times, just like Brigitte, the blonde girl two houses down the street. Brigitte was also an only child and about three years older than I. Doris, Inge, and Ursel, three girls who lived further up the street, were often in trouble. When Brigitte and I played outside in Brigitte's garden, we often heard these sisters screaming because their Daddy was whipping them. He was a member of the Party and wore a brown uniform with a swastika armband on certain days.

In addition to school, I also went to Sunday school at the Protestant church. I was "a little pillar of the church" and always knew my lessons.

My parents also took me to the theater for the Christmas pageant, which was like a world of wonder for me.

Having been called a Jew and becoming more and more aware of the growing anti-Semitism around us, I decided to concentrate on my studies and my Protestant Sunday school participation and to be a high achiever. In this way I hoped to earn the respect of my teachers and peers. This, however, was not easily done. These children, because of the misinformation they received in their homes and because of what they were told during our religious instruction, began to hate Jews and to call me names like "Christ killer."

Thus by the tender age of seven or eight, I became an outcast in the community. Most of the other children were not allowed to play with me. Can you imagine how I felt? The As I got for my schoolwork were only small comfort for the treatment I received outside the classroom. School was where I loved to be.

Things became worse in 1938, when at age ten I was enrolled in the "girls-only" school, the Goethe Lyceum, where Brigitte was also a student. Somehow my parents still found the money to send me there. We had to take the train to the city from our suburb. On the first day in this new school, our teacher asked questions about our religion. First the Protestant girls had to stand, then the Catholic girls, and finally the Jewish. One girl, Gisela Stern, stood up. I just raised my hand. This caused the teacher to start a lengthy interrogation. I tried to get things right and to explain my background, but no one seemed to understand. Hindsight told me that I should have just said *"Evangelisch"* (Protestant), but an earlier devastating experience with a very small lie had taught me that I must never tell a lie. From that day on, although I learned much and enjoyed my subjects, the other girls shunned me, and I always had to find the lowest girl in the class to share her desk with me in return for letting her copy from me. When the other girls walked arm in arm around the schoolyard, I sat alone on a bench during breaks. I withdrew more and more into my books and worked my way through my parents' small library of German classics. After a few months, Gisela disappeared from our class because of new Nazi laws regarding the schooling of Jewish children. I was allowed to stay, but I was isolated, totally ignored, as if I did not exist. I was allowed to participate only in strictly educational work but not in anything else. Socially, I was totally excluded. None of the girls cared to associate with me, half Jewish, though they did not attack me or call me names as the children in the elementary school had done.

"Our neighbor said to me: 'she can't deny her origins,'" I heard my Mother report to my Dad. I wondered what she meant by that. Strange, nothing was ever explained, nothing made clear. At school, during religious instruction, the other children's eyes bored through me when the teacher discussed how the Jews crucified Christ. But I was not even born then. My Dad told me once that his Jewishness had run like a red thread through his life. He wanted his children to be better off than he had been. But was I?

Then came *Kristallnacht*, November 1938. Fortunately my father was not home. He had just left that day to help his brother, who had suffered from the pogrom the previous night in Cologne, about 80 kilometers (50 miles) away. Both he and his brother were decorated World War I veterans.

After the Nazi invaders entered our ground floor apartment, they first tried to persuade my mother to file for divorce. Just then my father phoned from Cologne. They screamed obscenities at him through the telephone and finally cut the wire. Then they destroyed our home. When my father returned the next day, he could see with his own eyes what the invaders had done. During all this I was terribly frightened. I screamed and screamed. They told me to be quiet. But when the actual destruction began, I froze into a huge scream. That moment was the moment of my emotional death. After that I could no longer cry, not even about my father's death, which occurred almost exactly one year later. It was as if there was a band of ice around my heart.

After that November night, my father was not allowed to continue his occupation. We lost our income, our money, and most of our possessions. We could not pay the rent any more. We had to move, and we found a place with a Jewish family in downtown Dortmund. We were assigned just one large room. At that time, nobody was talking as yet about going into hiding.

Following *Kristallnacht*, the Nazis continuously pursued my father. It seemed that some competitor had blackened his name. Therefore, my father left us and was on the run. He underwent several operations just to get hospital admission. He stayed mainly in Roman Catholic hospitals. Because of the constant harassment he experienced during this time, certain symptoms of some kind of disease developed and got progressively worse. The Nazis would not let him alone, not even in the hospital. Finally, he ended up with a rare disease called *Pemphigus*, which also developed in concentration camp inmates. It is something like the plague, but not infectious. His disease progressed rapidly. Yet the Gestapo was after him all the while, till he was on his death bed in the Jewish hospital in Cologne. My mother and I continued to live in Dortmund, visiting him regularly during his illness. He died there.

Since my mother was a gentile, there was no immediate danger that we would be deported to a concentration camp. Even so, she was often harassed. After my father's death, she was hauled before the Gestapo several times. Years later she told me that, standing before those somber gates, she was afraid that once she entered the building she would not come out alive. Inside, she made it clear that her husband, the Jew, was dead; they had succeeded in getting him to his early grave. Still they wanted to question his gentile widowed partner. Maybe he had been involved in a secret conspiracy. Had he any connection with "the elders of Zion"? But there was no trace of any Zionist organization to be discovered. My father had never been involved in any specific Jewish activity. He wanted to be—and was—an assimilated German, a military hero. They asked and probed, but there was nothing to be found. Yet my mother could not convince them that he had not been involved in any anti-Nazi organization, no matter how hard she tried. Nevertheless, in the end they let her go, and after that she never heard from the Gestapo again. They must have come to the conclusion that we had nothing to tell them, that we had no incriminating information or activity, and that we were just ordinary middle-class people.

But this was not the end our suffering. After *Kristallnacht* and my father's premature death the next year, we continued to live in Dortmund. My mother found employment and an attic apartment of three rooms. We survived, but not without danger. Our income was minimal. We were starving. We were devastated. My emotional life was frozen. I was not able to grieve for my dad.

About forty years later, I had a dream: sitting on an island, my mother and I were weeping oceans of tears. When I woke up, I knew that this dream had finally broken the ice band around my heart.

When I was in the elementary school, I got many *A*s. Some teachers would stand up for me and give me the marks I had earned. But in 1938 and 1939 in the girls' private school, I got no more than two *A*s on any report card, and they would always be on different subjects. My most consistent *A* would be in English. I was so far ahead of the rest of the students in English that it was hard for the teachers to deny me *A*s in it. I never complained about my marks, for I knew that the teachers too were being watched and had to be careful. Even with *B*s I was quite content. I still remained a student in good standing, so I was not too worried. But at the time of my father's death in 1939, all this changed. My marks went down.

After the Wannsee Conference[3] in 1942, a succession of new laws against Jews and half-Jews made survival ever more difficult for me. As early as 1935 in the first supplementary decree to the *Reich Citizenship Law*, a definition of what it meant to be a Jew had been given: a Jew was anyone with at least three full Jewish grandparents, or anyone with two full Jewish grandparents and who belonged to the Jewish religious community when the law was promulgated on September 15, 1935. According to this definition, I was not a Jew.

The law had more difficulty with the definition of the *Mischlings*, the ones who were of mixed origin. Finally it was agreed that there were *Mischlings* of first degree and of second degree. Having one Jewish parent, I belonged to the first category.

At the Wannsee Conference on the Final Solution, it was decided that all European Jews would be deported to the East to be liquidated and all half-Jews would be sterilized. The Wannsee Conference also legislated that no half-Jew (*Mischling* of first degree) was allowed to continue in the German educational system beyond grade eight. For me this meant the end of high school. Thus my formal schooling came to an end when I was 14. To be thrown out of school was to me and my mother another calamity.

In 1943 our little attic apartment was bombed out by the Allied Forces. It burned down and we were left with absolutely nothing. This was the fourth tremendous blow after *Kristallnacht*, my father's death, and my expulsion from school.

My first year out of school at age 14 was called a *Pflichtjahr* (duty year). I was lucky to become a domestic servant; the alternatives were factory worker or forced laborer. My mother, a Lutheran gentile, looked around for some clergyman who would be sympathetic. I had been an enthusiastic member of the Lutheran church, baptized and confirmed at the age of 14. A retired minister, Pastor Bosselmann, became my employer. He lived in Dortmund. I worked out of the basement of his two-story apartment. It was very hard for my mother to see her only treasured child reduced to the status of a cleaning girl. In the Germany of that time housecleaning was a job only for lower-class people. I served the pastor for one year. He was quite senile and did not understand much of what was going on. The one thing he cared about was getting his meals on time. For me this was yet another traumatizing experience. Still it was much better than a concentration camp.

The next year, I worked as junior clerk for a construction company. The future was coming. I felt that the Nazi regime would collapse one day soon. So I took all the night classes I could get. I took courses in shorthand, typing, French and Spanish. My four years of studying English in the private school had formed a good foundation for the study of other languages. Even though demoralized by the loss of my previous formal schooling, I worked like one possessed. I knew that nothing but work was my salvation now.

During my adolescent years I missed the normal interaction with children and adults. Books became my only reliable friends. I read the great literary works of German authors and others. My parents had a small but good library. Lessing—author of *Nathan the Wise*—and Schiller—heroic playwright, poet, and professor of history—became my heroes, my mentors and comforters. I think I would not have survived without this, my private world.

Finally liberation came. In April 1945 the Americans arrived in Dortmund, and a few days later a British military government was set up. My ad hoc job was that of a street interpreter. My four years of English were of great help.

Postwar policies made my mother eligible for a widow's pension, but I received only a small sum of money in compensation for educational losses. My mother and I went to the military government to complain about a Nazi who had lived in the same house where we had resided in the attic. The Nazi had stolen our last bits of property stored in the basement, mostly feather bedding. We tried to get some redress, but I soon found out that these British officers did not want to hear anything about persecuted Jews and survivors of persecution.

Still our trip paid off. Noticing that I spoke very good English, the officers asked me whether I could type and take shorthand. They then asked me to work for them, which I did. I remained in my new job for about five years. In 1950 I decided to move from Dortmund to Frankfurt, where I got a job with *American Airlines* and later with the Canadian consulate.

Eventually I decided to migrate to Canada. My mother came the next year, but she did not like her experience here and did not want to consider remarriage. So she went back to Germany. I brought her over a few more times, but she always returned to Germany. In 1967 she was killed in a car accident in Canada during her last visit.

In 1952 I married a native Torontonian. He, too, came out of a bad situation. He had suffered during the years of the depression and his father was an alcoholic. He was a gentile. We both had become Unitarians. Our marriage lasted for only six years. We were not happy most of the time. This was to be expected, for we both had to rush through so many difficulties and to solve so many problems. After he got his M.D. and his diploma in psychiatry, he moved out and took our two children along. He had an income now, partly thanks to my help, but I was left alone, as alone as before.

When I came to Canada in 1952, I had no more than an eighth-grade education. In Germany I had earned a *Chamber of Commerce Interpreter's Diploma*, but that was of no use in Canada. I worked as a secretary, supporting my husband in his efforts to get his medical degree. I was the working immigrant and the wife of a student husband. After my husband left me in 1958, it took me a full year to determine what to do next. I was quite depressed.

In 1959 I enrolled in the University of Toronto in a General Arts program with a major in English. I did very well and graduated with a B.A. in 1962. I continued to study and, with the help of some scholarships and part-time teaching, I received my Master's degree in 1964.

In 1966 I became a lecturer in English at the recently established University of Waterloo. I taught there for 30 years till my retirement in 1996. I received my doctorate in English from the University of Toronto in 1971.

Looking back on my life, I note the perpetual inner conflict of one trying to be an ordinary Protestant child in an environment which stigmatized me as a Jew. In his early years my father had broken off his engagement with a Jewish girl and was happy to find in my mother a gentile companion. It was his hope that this would result in a better and easier life for his children than he himself had. But this hope did not become true. Like many other Jews and half-Jews, I considered myself very much to be a German. Had I considered Judaism in my adolescent years, I am sure that this would have made my father extremely unhappy.

After I found my career and place in Waterloo, I started to think more about my father's Jewish roots. In 1982 I organized the *Committee on Jewish Studies and the Holocaust* at the University of Waterloo. In 1983

I read a paper titled "We Too Are Survivors" at the Holocaust Remembrance Day.

I do think that all the suffering of the Jews was instrumental in the establishment of the State of Israel. You run when the fire behind you burns hot or when you feel the points of a pitchfork attacking you in the back. Had there not been a Holocaust, my mother and I would have kept on living in Germany and we would have lived a "normal life" (whatever this might have been) in Germany.

But now I enjoy living in Canada. There was a time when I had difficulty speaking German. I tried to get away from that language as far as possible. When I observed how my mother's friends tried to cover up what had happened and denied any responsibility (we are all Germans together and don't talk about those things), I became rather bitter and angry.

I cannot accept anti-Semitism. In 1986 I received an anonymous anti-Semitic poem from one of my students. I became very angry. I read it to my class. Fortunately my students were very supportive of me.

When I reflect on my life, I note that it has not been easy. At times I am still angry and bitter about my sufferings. Yet I am determined that my sufferings shall not have been in vain. I was with my parents' blessing a youthful "pillar" of the local Protestant church, but I was persecuted as a Jew, a *Mischling*. I rejected Christianity at the age of 16, in 1944. It was of no help to me, but this did not cause me to turn to Judaism, which to me is a very patriarchal religion. I became a Unitarian in 1951. But, at the age of 60, I returned to my childhood Lutheran denomination, ready to work toward a reconciliation of Judaism and Christianity. I now call myself once more a Lutheran, a Judeo-Christian.

History does not do justice to you when, blow after blow, your home is invaded and destroyed, your loving, caring, and faithful father is hunted to an early death, your schooling is ended abruptly, and the concentration camp looms as a possibility daily. History cannot tell how you freeze to ice and turn to stone. So, what then is history?

Like many other survivors of the darkest night of human history, I too have attempted to find words to express some reasons why this must never happen again. NEVER AGAIN! I believe we must continue to search for ways beyond this enormous historic tragedy.

I began with a quotation of Martin Luther's Reformation hymn. My comfort is still "A mighty fortress is our God," words which often have strengthened me against my encircling enemies: "they cannot win the day."

Notes

1 Although I learned much later that Luther's diatribes against the Jews have contributed to the sufferings of my family and myself, I found much comfort in this hymn, which I learned at Sunday school. The fourth stanza, from which the opening quotation was taken, reads in English:

God's Word forever shall abide,

No thanks to foes, who fear it;

For God himself fights by our side

With weapons of the Spirit.

If they take our house,

Goods, fame, child, or spouse,

Wrench our life away,

They cannot win the day.

The Kingdom's ours forever!

– *Lutheran Book of Worship*

(Minneapolis: Augsburg Publishing House, 1978), number 228.

2 Theresienstadt, several kilometers northwest of Prague, Czechoslovakia, was a ghetto established in 1941. It was described by Nazi propaganda as a pleasant "retirement" community for elderly Jews. In fact, it was a collection center for deportations. Even apart from massive deportations from Theresienstadt to eastern death camps, tens of thousands of Jews died at Theresienstadt.

3 The Wannsee Conference was named for the resort/conference center in southwestern Berlin where it was held in January 1942.

chapter twelve
DAVID & GENIA LUPA'S STORY

My name is David Lupa, and I was born in 1908 in Kolo, a medium-sized town in central Poland. I went to three different trade schools and became a tailor. I became so experienced that I could estimate a client's measurements exactly right just by looking him over.

During the thirties we heard more and more about the persecution and killing of the Jews in Germany. In 1939 at age 31, I became very much afraid of Hitler's Germany. I was quite sure that the Nazis would invade Poland. We were told that there would be more freedom for us Jews in Russia. So I left Poland illegally. But when I came to Russia, I was immediately arrested. I was forced into making confessions and condemned to five years of hard labor in Siberia. That was a terrible journey. I was transported in a cattle boxcar of a long train. It took three days and three nights to reach the work camp. I had no warm coat; I was wearing my shirt and my only pair of pants. I was in that car with other fugitives. Nobody gave us water or bread. The walls of the car were white from frost. For a toilet we had only a hole in the floor. We huddled close together to remain warm. Being young, we survived somehow.

In the camp we had to cut wood in a forest some 30 kilometers [20 miles] away. Every day we had to walk there and back. Mid-way we were allowed a short rest. Often they would wake me up at 3 a.m. to press me into making more confessions. They did not trust me since I was a Polish citizen and now also an illegal immigrant.

Many Canadians still seem to think that Stalin was better than Hitler, but both were evil men. I often wondered whether Hitler had learned his tactics from Stalin or Stalin from Hitler.

I was in Russia for six years and four months. I often prayed to God that He would give me so much bread that for once I would not be hungry. I dreamt about eating as much as I wanted, about seeing a sign: "All you can eat." I had to do hard labor. Once each day I received a portion of black bread, which had a rubbery taste, and some sour pickles. My health suffered. Twice I had typhus and once malaria.

I was from a strict religious upbringing. While I was working in that labor camp in the bush, the greatest Jewish holiday, Yom Kippur, was coming. I told another Jewish man that I wanted to keep this holiday if at all possible. There were many Jews in that camp, and many others also wanted to celebrate Yom Kippur. I went to our guard, who also was a Jew, but his wife was a Gentile. He asked me to get the names and signatures of those who wanted to keep this holiday. So I did. When I returned to him with the list of names, he took it and started screaming at me. He cursed me terribly. He yelled, "How can you still believe in God? You must be against communism! Forget about your religion and your Yom Kippur. Only Stalin is God. Only father Stalin gives you bread!"

I go so scared that I could not sleep for a couple of nights. And then to know that this man was a Jew—I could not believe it. For me this was almost the end of my religion. When I prayed, I made sure that nobody saw it. Somehow I still believed in God. Some people ask me: "Where was God in those years? Was God still alive or was He dead?" I believe God was still alive and still there.

But many people were sinning greatly. Before 1939 crime increased in all of Europe and in the whole world. Many banks collapsed and went bankrupt. There was much prostitution, poverty and hunger, and much killing. When God punishes the bad people, the good people suffer with them and for them. It is written in the our holy books that in the end of time there will be only 36 righteous people in the whole world. It is written in the Good Book: "Never say, 'this man is bad, for he is rich and healthy'." You are not allowed to judge. Rather, suffer for him. The one suffers for the other. In this way the Jews were suffering for the sins of the world.

In the prisons, work camps, and concentration camps many died. I was fortunate. I survived and so did Genia, who later became my wife. I am thankful. Millions were dead, but we were still alive.

In 1942, after I had been in Siberia for about two years, I suddenly was told that my arrest and imprisonment had been a mistake. I was free. They put me on a train that first went far south and then traveled slowly north till I reached Stalingrad.

In 1945 when the war was almost over, I was in a hospital, suffering from dysentery. I was very weak by that time. So "they" decided that I should be killed. The doctors there practiced euthanasia. I was supposed to be given a lethal injection. People like me got this injection in the morning, and by the evening they were dead. On the day before I was to receive my injection, I left my hospital bed, sick as I was. I found my clothes and turned my face to God in prayer. I waited for an opening to escape. After about half an hour I heard a man yelling: "Lupa, Lupa!" I did not dare to answer, for I was very scared. Yet, somehow he found me. He told me that I would not be killed. The war was over and I would be free. The next day I left that hospital as a free man. But I could hardly walk. My feet were badly swollen. Someone brought me to a ship that went down the river. When the boat trip ended, I was close to a train station. There they gave me a free ticket to travel to Rostov. I think that ticket was free because the war was over and everybody was happy.

After some time, I came to Rostov, and the authorities there gave me permission to stay. The first few days I slept in the train station under a wooden bench. Like father Jacob (Genesis 28:11), I used a stone for a pillow. I had some bread which I had taken along from the hospital. For a piece of bread—people there were hungry too!—I bought a towel, which I draped over the stone pillow.

I needed better accommodations, so the next day I started looking for an apartment. When I rang the bell at a certain house, the lady who lived there asked what my profession was. I told her I was a tailor. She said I could rent a room at her place. She also brought me the materials to make a coat for her. For this I got my room rent free for the first month. She was a good lady. She washed my shirt which I had been wearing for five and one half months.

In 1946 I finally was sufficiently recovered to make the trip back to Poland. I went back to Kolo only to find out that my parents were dead and about one hundred of my relatives. Most of them had died in the gas chambers. There was nobody left for me in Kolo except for one sister, who now lives in Toronto. So I moved to Czestochowa, a fairly large city. I went back to the clothing business. To get started I sold my overcoat. But soon I had my own store specializing in women's coats and dresses. In 1952 I married Genia, with whom I have now been married for 34 years.

Before I tell you the rest of my story, which now becomes our story, let Genia first tell what happened to her before 1952.

Genia:

I was born in 1926. Like David I was born in Poland, but on the other side, the eastern border, close to the Ukraine, in Diochobitz, a small town. Half of the people living there were Jewish; the others were Gentiles.

In 1939, when I was 13, the war broke out. The Germans soon occupied Poland, and they gave our area to the Russians. So we became a Russian territory for about two years. But in 1941 the war between the Russians and the Germans began. The Germans returned to Diochobitz and they promised the Ukrainians freedom. But as they returned, they killed some 160 Jews by stoning them to death. I found myself in the middle of that fight. Suddenly and miraculously there appeared a man in a black suit, who grabbed me and got me outside the area of the fight. He told me to go home. I still don't know who he was or why he did it, but I am still thankful to him for saving me.

Living under German authority, we were moved into a ghetto, a special crowded area in the city we were not supposed to leave. Every few months some officer would come in and make a selection. People he thought were not fit to work any more had to stand to his left side to be liquidated. The Germans never "killed" Jews; they only "liquidated" or "terminated" them! I was still healthy and strong and could work in war machinery factories. I was hungry most of the time. Food was a luxury and became ever more scarce.

Soon the ghetto changed into a concentration camp. Every day we received some soup and bread, but not much. Happily, we still had some money. The Gentiles took our gold watch and our rings in exchange for food. So we survived. During my stay in that concentration camp, the Gestapo put me to work in their garden. I had to work in the greenhouse caring for the tomatoes, but I was not allowed to touch them.

I was in the concentration camp from 1941 until May of 1944, when the Russians liberated us. In the meantime most of us had gone to the death camp. From the 500 in 1941 only 60 of us were left in 1944. When the time came that my mother and I would also be liquidated, I just walked away from the camp. My mother was sure that a German officer would shoot me. But he didn't. Somehow still later my mother also escaped with a niece.

Because I did not look very Jewish, I passed several policemen and they let me go. I went to the house of a Ukrainian man of whom I had heard. He had a large cellar under his house, where he was hiding 49 Jews. In his house upstairs lived two German officers who were not supposed to know that we were there in hiding. This Ukrainian man was not part of the resistance movement. He did it for money. In the end we were all out of money, but he still supported us and brought us food.

Our protector asked me whether I knew where my mother was. I said I did not. In the meantime my mother and her niece, whose parents had been killed by the Germans, escaped the concentration camp and were hiding in a bunker. The Germans were looking for them with bloodhounds, but another lady who also was hiding there had paprika and put that around the opening near the door. So the dogs lost the smell of us. After I had been in my hideout for some time, my mother walked in with my niece and a little baby. We stayed in hiding for about four-and-a-half months until the Russians liberated us in September 1944. But we had no place to go to. There was hardly any food, so we went back to the concentration camp and stayed there for about one year. The Germans were only about three kilometers [two miles] away. The Russian soldiers were good to us. They gave us food and coffee and even a piece of sugar. But after a while they told us to leave the camp and find an apartment in the city. I took a job in a Russian restaurant, which gave us food to eat. I stayed there for about one year.

In 1945 we returned to Poland. My mother had heard from her son, who wrote that my father was still alive. We looked for them, but someone told us that both of them had left for Germany. So we traveled west. Then one day as we were changing trains, I exclaimed, "There is my father! Father!" My mother first thought I had gone crazy. But sure enough it was he. He was very skinny and weak. So all together we went back to Poland, to the city of Czestochowa. We found an apartment and started a new life. Free at last. Soon everyone went to work. But my mother developed serious heart trouble and died in 1951.

Then in 1952 I met David and we got married. That is now 34 years ago. David will tell you what happened next.

David continued:

The rest of our story can be told quickly. In 1957 we left Poland for Israel. We felt very strongly that the Jews needed their own country. There should never be a Holocaust again. Any garden needs a fence. If there is no fence, the pigs come in and destroy the garden. Without land of their own the Jews will again be destroyed. We lived in Tel Aviv for two years and nine months. I had a clothing store. But I could not stand the climate. It was too hot and humid, too tropical. So we left.

We moved to Canada. When I arrived, I kissed the ground. In April 1960 we came to Kitchener and I started my own business on King Street, David's Men's Wear. Now, in 1986, we are almost ready to retire. I have angina pectoris, and Genia had a heart attack five years ago.

When we retire, we may be able to help some other refugees or poor people. During all these years God has been good to us. We have kept the faith. We attend the services in the Synagogue. I don't eat or drink without my skull cap. We are happy that we can practice our religious belief in freedom. We became Canadian citizens. I already spoke Polish, Russian, and German; and after 1960 I learned English in my store to serve my customers. Yes, we are looking forward to our retirement and will find something worthwhile to do.

Postscript: In 1990 both David and Genia died.

chapter thirteen
THEODORE MILO'S STORY

I was born on December 7, 1925, in Krosniewice, Poland. Originally my name was Tovi Milosierny, but I changed that in Canada to Theodore Milo. I never changed my name in the work camps or later in the concentration camp. Once there, I became just a number. Here it is on my forearm: 144342. When after the war my children noticed it and asked me what the number meant, I often just responded: "It used to be my telephone number."

[*Ed. note:* Theodore's wife, Betty, added, "Theodore never wants to talk about the war and camp time. He never told me what happened to him. Other people told me how he suffered.]

I still don't like to talk about it. I just wanted to go on with my life. Never before have I consented to be interviewed. But it comes back to me in my dreams. More than once I thought I would not survive.

I was the fifth of six children. My father was a tailor. Working hard, he managed to provide for our family. Compared with others, we were not that bad off. We certainly were not rich or even well to do, but many others were much poorer than we.

Before the war, the Jews in Krosniewice lived among the Gentiles, but in 1939 the Germans occupied the city, and, after a few months, all the Jews had to live in a ghetto. I was fourteen at that time. Soon thereafter, we had to work for the Nazis, cleaning the streets and shoveling snow. But this did not last very long. The next year, I was sent away from home to a workcamp. I stayed there for about two years. In 1942 I was transported to another workcamp. There too the work was heavy. We built roads for the German army. But this ended abruptly. In 1943 the Germans sent us to a concentration camp, to Auschwitz, and there right away I got my number. Our work was hard. Fortunately, my health remained good. I went through quite a number of selections, but obviously I always made it; otherwise I would not be here today.

I remained in Auschwitz till January 1945. The Russians were close by, but the Germans did not want to let us go. Thus, in the middle of winter with freezing temperatures, we had to walk about 40 kilometers [25 miles] to Gleiwitz. There we were put on a train, in cattle cars. First we went southwest, and so we came to Austria. In Vienna we saw people going to work. Some tried to share their bread with us. But soon the guards stopped this humanitarian gesture. From Vienna we went north to Dora [in central Germany], which is where they made the V1 and the V2 rockets. Engineers and scientists there were also working on the atom bomb. We worked in Dora from January through March 1945.

I knew by then that the war was coming to an end. The Russians were approaching from the East and the allied forces from the West. But again the Germans did not want us to stay there, in Dora. They did not want us to be liberated. Being Jews, we should be "terminated." So they found another train, and we ended up in Hamburg [in northwest Germany]. The plan was to put us on an old boat and, once at sea, sink the ship and thus kill us.[1] But the mayor of Hamburg and many people in the community had had enough of the atrocities of the war and were also very much aware of having to face the day of reckoning. Therefore, they tried hard to save their skins by "rescuing" some of us after having killed millions.

I remember an interesting incident from that time. While we were still in Auschwitz preparing for the long march to Gleiwitz, some of my old buddies from my home town tried hard to persuade me to stay with them. They thought I would be safer if I joined them. But I refused. I told them that I had a brother to care for and would not leave him. My buddies got to Hamburg ahead of me and were drowned at sea. Once again I survived.

The Hamburgers did not want us to stay in their city, so we went back to the train. In an open box car they transported us from Hamburg to Bergen-Belsen [about 80 kilometers (50 miles)]. We were there for only two weeks when we were liberated.

With liberation also came food. It was a blessing that we could eat again till the hunger pains were gone. During the war years we had always been hungry. In the concentration camp of Auschwitz I became quite sick and went to the hospital barracks. Somehow I recovered and when freedom came, I was not sick anymore. I do not remember I was suffering from during my camp years. However, I became ill again after the war and my immigration to Canada. Soon I went to see a doctor in Toronto. I was amazed to discover that this physician had obtained the records of my previous illness when I was imprisoned in the concentration camp. You see, the Germans are very meticulous in keeping records.

I also remember that, while I was in that camp hospital, some German doctors told us to get out of there as soon as possible, since otherwise we most likely would be sent to the gas chamber. This helped amazingly much to heal us quickly! Some German doctors meant well and tried to protect us. The gas chambers were not in Auschwitz, but in Birkenau, which is very close [about two kilometers west]. When we went out to work, we often saw people being marched to the gas chambers, naked.

I was in Bergen-Belsen when the British liberated us, and I stayed there for another five years until it was closed. Then I was transported to another camp, Lubeck [in northern Germany]. Finally, in 1951, I boarded a ship in order to go to Canada. Since my cousin, Mr. Kay, was living in Kitchener, Kitchener is where I went.

I became a steelworker, and I like my work. In 1957 I married Betty Currie. She is not Jewish but of Scottish descent. She has not experienced the Holocaust. She came to Kitchener from Nova Scotia. We fell in love and married and were blessed with two children, a son and a daughter. They both went to the university and are married now. Our daughter took a course on the Holocaust. She is married to a Jewish man from Philadelphia. Both of our children observe the high holidays. They know they are Jews and want to remain Jews. Our daughter keeps a strict kosher home, and Betty does this too, though she was not born Jewish. Knowing that I had lost so many of my relatives, she wanted our children to be educated as Jews in the Jewish faith. "It's all he has," she used to say.

My father died in Auschwitz. My mother, my sister, my younger brother—they were all gassed and killed. Only my oldest brother is still alive. He lives in New York, but everybody else is dead. I used to have an uncle in Kitchener, but he died too. All I have here is Mr. Kay, a second cousin, and I am very close to him. I also still have some cousins in Jerusalem, but I don't know them. When our daughter studied in Jerusalem, she met them. I have some distant relatives in England, but I have no contact with them either.[2]

Betty has lots of relatives. We used to go to Nova Scotia every year to visit them.

Let me tell you also about my religious life. My parents were very religious, very observant Jews. My father was a member of the council of the synagogue. We went to the synagogue every day and celebrated all the Jewish holidays.

When the Germans came, I was just 14 years of age. I had had seven years of public school and some years of Jewish school. My Jewish teacher took us to Seder, and I was able to read the Siddurs, but that was the extent of my knowledge of the Hebrew language.

In the camps we could not practice our religion. Sometimes I prayed or tried to pray, but it was very hard. Often we felt forsaken by God. We all asked, "Where is God?" Our rabbis tried to answer our questions and help us. But at the selections they were usually chosen first and disappeared. Even though we Jews did not have an easy time in Poland before the war, in the camps it was so much worse.

Yet I still believe in God. Some people may say that God is dead, but I don't accept that. I know we suffered very much. We are God's suffering servant from Isaiah 53. If there were prizes for suffering, the Jews would deserve the first prize!

Auschwitz may have helped the Jewish people to establish a Jewish homeland in Israel. O yes, I would not mind living in Israel. If I had gone there straight from Germany, it might have been O.K. But for us, after our Canadian years, it would have been very difficult.

I still have great fear of uniforms. If a policeman stops me, I freeze. I even have a problem crossing the border to the U.S.A. I also will never watch the October parade. Sometimes I find it difficult not to hate German people, but I know I cannot blame a whole nation for what happened to us. However, war criminals such as Joseph Mengele should be punished.

Maybe Betty wants to add something to my story?

Betty responded:

Yes, I know how difficult it is for Theo to talk about these things. He never wanted to be interviewed. Sometimes Theo still has nightmares about his camp time. But he is a strong believer. My faith is not that strong. When I hear all these camp stories, I wonder whether there is a God. Even though I too believe in God, I ask myself: 'Where was God then?' I don't know the answer.

I have strong feelings of justice. During the war time and afterwards, we had Mackenzie King as our prime minister. But when Jews during and after the war tried to come to Canada, he would not grant them permission to land here, and in the United States of America exactly the same thing happened. It seems that in government circles, there was not much compassion for suffering people.

I still shudder when I think of all the injustice of the past. It is perhaps for this reason that I did not find it difficult to give up my Protestant Christian tradition and to accept the Jewish faith. I definitely wanted our children to be Jews.

Notes

1 The same death by drowning had been planned for Remkes Kooistra's father; see the chapter titled "My War Years."

2 Many survivors of the Holocaust try to reconstruct, as much as possible,

their family tree. The remnant seeks expansion towards the future. Children are very welcome. It is important that there be not only the individual survival but also a collective one.

chapter fourteen
JACK & MIRIAM SOMER'S STORY

This is the story of Mr. and Mrs. Somer as told on October 20, 1986. We listened first to Jack's story.

My name is Jack and my wife's name is Miriam. We live in Kitchener, Ontario. I was born on November 20, 1929, and Miriam on April 15, 1928. We were both born in the same city, Radziejew, in Poland.

In 1939 Germany invaded Poland. We knew of all kinds of terrible things the Nazis were doing to the Jews in Germany, so the whole family decided to run. After a while, we ended up in a smaller city, Debrowice. Some of our relatives were living there too. It was here that the Germans caught up with us. Immediately we had to wear the Jewish star. In 1941 the Germans took me and my brother to a so-called "civilian work camp" in Szocrode. We worked in that camp for about two years. But then in January 1943, the Germans rounded up all Jews from the work camps and transported them to Auschwitz, which at that time was still considered to be part of Poland.

I lost my brother in Auschwitz. This is how it happened. We had been newcomers to the work camp in Szocrode. So we were assigned to the heaviest labor: we had to pull cables. Those cables were pulled by some 300 men. My brother was a tall fellow, so he had also to pull for the short fellow standing beside him. If that cable did not move fast enough according to the German guard, he whipped my brother. This went on for about six months. In the end he was beaten up so often and so badly that he never completely recovered from his wounds. They sent him to Auschwitz because he could no longer do hard labor. And there he perished even before I arrived there. I never saw him again after he was sent away from Szocrode.

I also had a twin sister and an older sister. They too were sent to Auschwitz, and they perished there.

I, however, survived Auschwitz somehow. Finally it was January 1945. Now Auschwitz, as you know, was close to the Russian border. At that time the Russian army was marching up to Auschwitz. Why did the Germans not let us just become Russian prisoners? They had hardly any equipment left and yet they transported us, Jews, who were anyway condemned to die, away from the front. I could not understand why they did this. Were we still of any use to them at this time? Did they not realize that they had lost the war?

It was terribly cold that January 1945. The Germans took us first on a forced march to Gleiwitz, about 40 kilometers (25 miles) northwest from Auschwitz. Those who could not keep up with the march were just shot or left behind to die along the road.

Finally we came to Gleiwitz, where we remained for two or three days, until they found a train for us. They loaded us on this cattle train, one hundred people per box car. We had just enough room to stand. We were chilled to the bone. The train moved on and on, and eventually we arrived in Prague, Czechoslovakia.

Sometimes, even in the most terrible days, there is a bit of luck. This is what happened in Prague. We stopped under a bridge. Many of the people in our car were already frozen to death. We who were barely alive picked up a corpse and showed it to the Czech workmen as they passed by en route to their factories. Many of them threw their lunches to us in the open box car. Those who were strong enough caught the food and had, once again, something to eat. Food was life.

Later, the train moved again. It seemed even colder than before. Of the one hundred men in our wagon only half were still alive. In the night it became even colder than in daytime. We used the dead bodies as blankets to keep ourselves warm. I also had put some bodies under me and picked up yet another frozen body to cover me. Suddenly its head turned around and said: "I am not dead yet." Of course, I hastily put him down beside me, but a few hours later he was dead anyway. I will never forget this incident. I can still hear his slow voice. I still see his ashen-faced head turning on his frozen body, which I thought was already a corpse.

In the end, we arrived at Buchenwald. Of the original one hundred in our wagon, only fifteen were still alive. The others were dead. The whole journey was sheer madness, a death ride.

I stayed in Buchenwald for only four or five weeks. We then were sent to another work camp. Here we worked underground, producing airplanes. The factory was a huge dug-out in the mountain. While I was there, I thought I was going to die soon. I was very weak and we had very little food. One day they asked for volunteers still to go to yet another camp. Since I had nothing to lose, I thought I might as well go there. By this time my feet were so swollen I could hardly stand or walk. I realized that if the fluid were to reach my heart I would die.

Again I had to board a train for departure. Because we had volunteered, we got a chunk of bread. Bread was life, a chance to last a bit longer. This train moved to the east, to Magdenburg. On our way British war planes came over and the pilots thought we were a transport of soldiers. They attacked us. Many of us died, hit by the bullets of our liberators.

During the attack something happened which shows what hunger can do to people. One of us was a barber from Warsaw. As the train was moving, he said, "I may as well eat this bread now. I may be dead later." (Others were saving most of it.) During the air-attack, a bullet hit him in the head. He died immediately. But a piece of bread was still in his mouth. Bread was life. One of us prisoners took the bread out of the barber's mouth and ate it. We were all hungry, hungry all the time. Always we were looking for food. We became hunting animals. We lost all human dignity.

And so we arrived in Magdenburg. Here we marched to work, though I could hardly walk. We had to clean up the rubble from the air attacks. I had to clean bricks. Happily I could sit down doing this. Others, who were still stronger, were able to dig and often they found some food in bombed out shelters and in cellars of big buildings. The potatoes we found were burned from the fires, but still it was food. Our whole life had become a search for food. We survived in what was left of that city. We even took some food home to the camp and cooked it in the evening. I was only fifteen years old at that time. This helped me to recover. My strength increased.

We worked there until April 1945. The war came to its end. Russian and American armies approached the city from the east and the west. But again the Germans did not want us to be captured by the "enemy." So they marched us out of our camp. After a few hours we stopped at a field for a short rest. Then the Americans flew over and bombed us. Many of us died. We would all have died if the Americans had not finally recognized our striped prison uniforms which we were frantically waving at them. This was the moment of confusion for which I had been waiting. I ran.

I fled into the woods. Quite a few others also escaped and were hiding there. Soon I met some of them. I went to a house and stole some civilian clothes. A short while later I saw a civilian, whom I recognized as another prisoner. He was originally from Greece. I had met him in Buna, the work camp near Auschwitz. There we had developed a kind of sign language to communicate. So I gave him the sign for Buna. He said, "Yes," he had been there. So we decided to form a team.

We noticed that the SS-men were still hunting for prisoners who had escaped during the American attack. So we ran. We ran deeper and deeper into the woods. European woods are much easier to cross than Canadian. Deep into the woods we found many more people in hiding. They were from all over Europe, from every nationality. We all knew that the war was coming to an end. So we kept on running, afraid to be captured, seeking safety and shelter. There were even some German soldiers among us. These deserters knew that Hitler had lost the war. The first thing I did was to grab a gun. But I did not yet know how to shoot. One day the SS-ers came very close to where we were hiding. They hollered and shouted for us to come out. But we did not. For we were scared. Happily they did not find us and we marched on.

After some time, we reached the river Elbe. We came to the city Torgau. This is where the Americans and the Russians met. Here we were liberated. It felt wonderful to be again a free man. But even this was not to be the end of my story of survival.

I stayed together with my Greek friend. We were still hungry and always looking for food. The Russians took over the command of Torgau and put to work anybody who was still able to move. But I was in no physical condition to help clean up the city. Then I met another ex-prisoner from Poland. I told him that I wanted to go home, to Poland. He too wanted this. So we took off again and started marching east. On the east side of the Elbe we went from village to village. Somewhere we picked up a bicycle, which was a great help. Finally we ran into a Russian road block. These Russian soldiers asked as where we were going. We said: "We are going home." They took as along to a Prussian farm house, where they were stationed. They gave us uniforms and said: "Now you are Russian soldiers, now you belong to the victorious Russian army!"

Here we stayed for a while. We worked with the Russians. I put on weight. I thought: "I am going to be fat!" One night the Russians came in with food. I took a dozen eggs, a chunk of butter and perhaps a couple of kilograms (about a pound) of the Russian black bread with a glass of vodka. While I was eating all this, a bunch of Russian soldiers looked at me in amazement. But it seemed that my stomach was a bottomless pit. I did not get sick from this big meal. I think the vodka helped too.

One day I met a Russian lieutenant. He was a wonderful person. He said, "Jack, if you stay here, you will never get home and find out what happened to your family." He told me that he with a number of soldiers would take horses through eastern Germany and Poland to Russia. He told me in which villages they would stop for the night. So, after they had left the next day, I ran again and caught up with his group in a nearby village. The lieutenant promised me that he would bring me home. In my Russian uniform, I went to a German farmer and asked him to hitch up a couple of horses for me. He obeyed for he was scared. The roles had been reversed. I was now in command. I had a gun. With the horses and the cart, I joined the lieutenant and his men on my way to Poland.

As we moved on from village to village a funny thing happened to me. You see, not all Russians are bad people, not even all Germans. As we entered a village near the Polish border, I heard behind me the voice of our commanding officer saying "Hey Jack, I see you, but I don't see you any more." I took this as a sign to run. And run I did. Some soldiers went after me, but they gave me a break. I escaped. And so, finally, I was free and back in Poland.

First of all I went to my hometown Radziejew to find out if anybody there was still alive. There were some survivors. They told me that an uncle of mine was alive and living in Czentowa. So I went there to meet him. I talked to him but soon I discovered that I could not stay in Poland. Hardly any of our Jewish people were left. It felt awful to have no relatives anymore, no friends, no community. I left and went to East Germany and thus I moved from the Russian to the American zone. After much waiting and working in the meantime, I was allowed in 1947 to emigrate to the United States. It was not easy. Yet somehow I got in contact with a group working for the United Nations and they sponsored a large number of young people from different nationalities. They took us to the United States; we did not need a passport. In Buffalo, NY, I learned my trade as a furrier and worked for 11 years. But first I had to learn the English language. I went for two years to an evening high school and graduated. In the beginning, I worked in the fur shop as a floor boy. But after about ten years, I ran the shop. In 1958 I had a chance to go to Israel and there I met Miriam, whom I married. I was twenty nine by that time.

Now Miriam told her story:

I too was born in Radziejew, in Poland. My date of birth is April 15, 1928. So at the beginning of the war in 1939, I was just eleven years old. My parents were scared too, and we fled from Radziejew to Kowal, and from there we went to Czenstowa, which was supposed to be located in the free part of Poland. But soon the Germans came there too and took over. We ended up in a ghetto.

After a while, we were brought to a concentration camp. My mother had to work there in hard labor. But then the time came that she could not do it anymore. I knew that soon they would make another selection. Those who were directed to the left side would be brought to Germany to be liquidated. I knew my mother would be one of the first ones to go. I myself was in another barracks. The Gestapo came into the camp with their blood hounds and when they discovered people who were hiding, they would shoot them right there. I could have run away. But I did not want to leave my mother. Someone helped her to escape. From her hiding place, she went to the factory where I had been working. But she found out that I was not there anymore. I was in the camp in my barracks. That is where my mother went too to visit me. But the guards did not let her come in. She begged them, "Please, let me in. I want to be with my daughter."

The answer was "NO!"

Mother tried again to get in. They beat her. But she kept on asking, imploring, begging. Finally one Nazi showed some pity. He said, "Come on, let her in, no big deal." So she returned to the camp and came to live with me in my barracks. But other prisoners noticed this too and they also wanted to have their relatives admitted. Then the Germans changed their mind. There was no more mercy. They announced that anybody who had come in from the outside had to come out. But my mother and I stayed where we were, hiding under a straw mattress.

Eventually, it became January 15, 1945. It was the day before our liberation. We heard the Russian artillery in the background. But we knew that we were not free yet. We used to say in the ghetto and later in the concentration camps: "If the war will end at 12:00 noon, they will still finish us five minutes before 12:00 noon."

But on the 16th of January the Russians came in. We were, indeed, free. It was the greatest thing that could happen to us. Of course, we left the camp. Whatever we could find, we took along with us. We found some bread, some flour, potatoes and vegetables. Anything edible was welcome. It seemed that I had a stomach without bottom, just like Jack.

I stayed with my mother. Soon I went back to high school. I was the only Jewish student in that school. There was still much anti-Semitism in Poland. There was the so-called "A-K" army. They were still trying to kill all the Jews. I remember that we were living close to a very nice restaurant. One night a young Jewish couple, just married, went there for their evening meal. As they came out of the restaurant, they were shot dead—just because they were Jews. In this way lots of Jews died in Poland, even after the war. My gentile Polish neighbor once said that what the Nazis did not finish she would gladly do.

Yes, there were some exceptions. There were people who sacrificed their own lives for the Jews. They were exceptions, but these too must be remembered.

Yet the majority of the people did not help us. When we ran for protection and safety, there were always Polish people waiting to rob our houses and take our possessions. They knew us and recognized us as Jews much easier than the Nazis did. They would report on us to the Nazis in exchange for food or personal advantage or even just for pleasure.

I graduated from high school, and in 1950 my mother and I went to Israel. There I learned Hebrew. I was twenty two by then. In 1958 I met Jack and we were married. After that, we went first to the United States and then to Canada.

I love studying. In Canada I took courses at Conostoga College, Kitchener, for three years. Later on I took courses at the University of Waterloo. I like psychology very much. I really wanted to know what makes Jews so different from the rest of mankind? And what about the Nazis? How did they become what they were? They also belonged somehow to the human race. These are some of the questions I still try to answer.

We did not have many relatives left after the war. I am happy to have still my mother. But Jack's parents died in the middle of the war, in 1943. They were sent from Auschwitz to nearby Helmna. There they went straight to the oven. They were gassed, terminated.

Jack found one uncle still alive after the war. He lived in Kitchener.

But he is not with us anymore; he died in 1981. Jack also has some second and third cousins there, who had come to the New World before the war. Having some of Jack's relatives here in Kitchener led us to move from the United States to Canada in 1958, shortly after our arrival in the New World.

I also have some relatives in Kitchener, two aunts and one cousin. I am very close to one of my aunts. And, of course, there is also my mother, who still lives with us and is now 83 years of age.

I have no relatives in Israel. And in Poland we have none left either. Everyone is gone. My sister was shot to death. My father too. Even my little cousin, who was hiding in a bunker, was killed after having been discovered. My uncle was hanged. I wonder how can some people still deny the reality of the Holocaust?

At this point, both Jack and Miriam answered our questions.

What can you tell us about the ghettos?
As soon as the Germans occupied Poland, they moved all Jews to one part of the city, which then was called a ghetto. We had no ghettos in Poland before the Germans came. But after they occupied the country there were ghettos in every city where Jews were living. All Jews had to wear the star.

First these ghettos were quite large. But soon the Nazis began with their selections. People who could not work anymore or were weak were selected out to be liquidated. You stood in line and had to go the one side or the other. The one side was for living, the other for dying. You never knew when the next selection would come. Every day could bring death. We did not even live day by day, but moment by moment. Soon the ghettos became smaller and smaller. We were imprisoned in the ghetto, waiting for death to come sooner or later.

How did your Polish neighbors react to all this?
Before the war we lived next to Gentiles. Their children were my friends.

I often slept in a gentile house and gentile friends were sleeping in our house. There were good Poles who wanted to protect us and condemned the ghettos. But they were in danger too and often they too were killed or murdered. Yet, the majority of the population did not react. They were Polish and used to unpredictability. There were no strikes like in the Netherlands. We had no organized resistance movement, though there were partisans living in the forest. But these groups were of mixed nationalities. In fact, they were not real partisans, rather fugitives, people who had escaped the system and tried to survive in the forest. After Jack ran away from the German transport, he too was in the forest, going toward the river Elbe in order to meet the Russians.

We never had false identification papers as in Germany or in other countries; we in Poland were not that well organized.

Did you lose money and possessions during the occupation?

Yes, very much so. When we escaped for the first time from Radziejew, we had nothing but the clothes we were wearing. We left everything behind. Our houses were robbed by Polish people. They did not expect us to return and thought perhaps that they might as well take what they could grab.

Did you suffer physically?

JACK: Yes, I was beaten many times. I had my teeth knocked out. Once I was given 15 lashes.

MIRIAM: I was slapped repeatedly. I remember one case quite well. I was working in the factory. I was on my knees, scrubbing the floor. Suddenly there appeared a young Polish man. He touched my back. I looked up. He told me that I was supposed to meet him at a certain time and place. I had never seen him before. I did not know who he was. But the other girls told me that he was the worst supervisor of all. He was a Polish collaborator. After a while he came back and told me to come with him. He took me along and told his Nazi supervisor that he wanted to punish me for being the laziest girl of them all. I got so angry. I spoke to the supervisor. I was trembling all over. I said: "How can he say that. He does not even know me. He never saw me before today. He does not have the right to say this!"

The Nazi started laughing. He had never seen a girl so angry. I was not supposed to feel any indignation. Then he said: "Go back to work!" This I gladly did. In the meantime I saw that the other man had taken out his whip, but he could not do anything since I was sent back to my floor. Yet, when the Nazi went inside after a while, the Polish man approached me again and slapped me twice on my face. "Take this," he hissed in anger.

I know that after the liberation he was on trial. I would have gladly given my testimony, but I was in another city at that time. I heard he got a life sentence. That is what he deserved.

JACK: During these years in the camps I was never really sick. The only problem I had was the swelling of my feet, which often made it difficult to walk. My sickness was hunger.

MIRIAM: I became sick in the concentration camp. I had high fever. I ended up in the hospital, which was actually only a barracks, not like a German hospital. It was dangerous too, because selections went on also in that so-called hospital. In my fever I started hallucinating. I had a large loaf of bread and a knife. Or I was a bird. I had wings and I could fly. I was neither a Jew nor a Pole. I was free. What a feeling! It is hard to comprehend what freedom meant to me.

Were there also times of relief in the concentration camp?
JACK: Yes, in Buna we had concerts. A band played as we marched to work. We had musicians from all over Europe. We had Poles, Russians, Dutch, Danish, and others. These concerts were actually not intended for us, but for the SS. They also brought in Greek prisoners, for the SS liked to watch men dancing, and in Greece men do this well and often. Sometimes they also had us play soccer for their entertainment.

Could you practice your Jewish religion while in camp?
JACK: I noticed some people still practicing their religion. Some

people had smuggled prayer books and prayer shawls into the camp. Several people still prayed, but those who were caught praying died on the spot by gunshot.

In 1944 we got some people in from Hungary. They refused to eat some kinds of meat like salami. "This is against our religion," they said.

But the old-timers talked them out of it. They told them, "You better eat this; it is your life!"

MIRIAM: We never knew when it was Sabbath. In the ghetto we observed Sabbath, but not anymore in the concentration camps. There it was impossible.

Are you observing Jews now? Do you attend services in the synagogue?

JACK: We are perhaps not as religious as we should be.

MIRIAM: We go to the synagogue on the major religious holidays, but not on Saturdays. At home we eat kosher, but not at the restaurants.

Question: Will the Jewish religion survive?

JACK: It always has. Many other religions have died. True, there are many different streams among us. We are not Hasidim. We don't wear a special kind of clothes.

MIRIAM: Yes, I see changes in our religious practices. Before the war, in Poland, we all followed the same pattern, the same practices. We, of course, were still children at that time and did not really understand why we did what we did. But now? We have seen that there are so many ways to be Jewish.

I remember that while I was in the camp in 1943, I made a promise to myself. I had heard one child asking: "What is it to be a Jew? What will they do to us because we are Jews?"

Another child said: "They will shoot us."

Someone explained, "Because we are Jews."

Then the child asked again, "Why?"

It was this "WHY?" which burned within me. Then I promised myself: "I will never judge people on their color, nationality, religion or anything else. I will judge people only on what they are."

JACK: There is also Zionism.

MIRIAM: But Zionism is not really a religion; it is basically a political ideology. But it is good to have Zionism. Without it we would not be today where we are now.

JACK: To have a country of your own is like having a father or mother! It means protection and identity. It's very important. Without parents any child is left alone.

Do you still believe in God?
MIRIAM: I do, but I don't understand God.

Was the holocaust a punishment from God?
JACK: A punishment for little children? I can't believe this.

MIRIAM: I don't know. Punishment for what? There are enough guilty people among us. The Nazis are not the only ones. The whole world is guilty. We all let it happen. Should we all be victimized by a holocaust?

Do you still have bitter feelings against the Germans?
JACK: First after the war, I was very bitter. But I found out that you cannot be bitter against everybody. Right after the war, I lived in Germany. Not all Germans are bad people. I have friends among them.

MIRIAM: I don't want to feel bitter. To feel bitter would still be a victory for the enemy. You cannot let anybody make you bitter because then you become the victim of your bitterness. Then you would be again a victim. We have been victims long enough. Bitterness is like a cancer: it eats the person who is bitter. It eats you, if you are bitter.

chapter fifteen
LASS' MICH STERBEN
[LET ME DIE]

by Jerzy Tadeusz Pindera

Night of Friday, 13 February 1942

The night was beautiful. Not a single cloud obscured the dark blue sky. I could clearly see the Great Dipper and, looking past the North Star, my favorite constellation, the Cassiopeia. Even the sharp glare of the searchlights regularly sweeping over the ten thousand men silently standing on the *Appellplatz* could not obscure this wonderful view, the enchantment of the deep winter sky filled with brilliant stars.

There was little snow on the *Appellplatz*, for no snow cover can survive the load of thousands of feet trampling over it. The soil was deeply frozen and rang when the men moved. On the Dead Zone, however, between the barbed wire entanglements and the electrified fence surrounding the camp, the snow was practically undisturbed. It was very cold, and so the snow in the Dead Zone sparkled brightly as the light beams of the powerful searchlights located above the entrance gate to the camp passed over it.

The cold was piercing, with the temperature at least 20 degrees Celsius below freezing [minus 4 degrees Fahrenheit]. Both the frost and the tense atmosphere suppressed in my mind any feeling of hunger and altered beyond belief my perception of time. Each second appeared to be as long as eternity—time seemed as frozen and still as the immobile men on the *Appellplatz*.

I remember glancing with a glimmer of hope at the large illuminated clock, just above the heavy machine guns up on the watchtower which straddled the entrance gate to the camp. The machine guns were trained on us—ten thousand men who stood quietly and obediently on the *Appellplatz*. The large hand just moved—it was 11:23 p.m. Just twenty-three minutes past eleven o'clock in the evening or one hour and twenty-three minutes after the time for going to sleep in the evening, but it seemed as if we had already stood on the *Appellplatz* for an infinitely long time. Almost six hours earlier the SS-Block-Leaders, called *Blockführers,* took reports from the Block-Elders, prisoners in charge of inmates of a barracks called Block, carefully checked the numbers of prisoners in the columns under their authority, and reported those numbers to the SS-Report-Leader of the camp. Every single man was accounted for, alive or dead, but we were not permitted to enter our barracks. We were being punished.

For the SS-Officers manning the machine guns above the entrance gate, high above our heads, the view must have been unique and in a sense full of a strange, brutal wonder. The entire inmate population was organized into more than fifty columns of prisoners called Blocks, like their barracks, each Block five rows deep, and each comprising two- to three-hundred immobile, mute men standing perfectly still. Behind the columns densely arranged on the *Appellplatz* there were several rings of timber barracks serving as living quarters, all snow-covered, dark and cold. Among those barracks there were some utility barracks, hospital barracks, a brick kitchen building, and a concrete penal building, called the Bunker, with facilities for special punishments and for more sophisticated and slow executions. The whole site was girdled by four rings of enclosures— a wide barbed-wire entanglement surrounded by an electrified fence three meters [about ten feet] high, followed by a concrete walk for the SS-Patrols with dogs specially trained for killing prisoners, and finally a concrete fence three meters high, topped with barbed wire. The monotony of this last solid fence was interrupted by several watchtowers equipped with heavy machine guns and powerful searchlights.

This view must have given the SS-Officers an immense feeling of power. A handful, a few dozen at most, of the SS-Guards manning the towers and another handful of the SS-Block-Leaders supervising the discipline on the *Appellplatz*, had the right to use their power of life or death over ten thousand men standing mute and immobile with expressionless faces and looking straight ahead.

I was there—a part of it all—and I could hardly escape a feeling of unreality. This was not the planet Earth as I knew it before. True—in spite of being a citizen of the twentieth century, brought up in a humanistic and liberal atmosphere of a progressive society with some feudal traditions—I had already learned to acknowledge the existence and the standards of behavior of the SS-members. Thus I was forewarned and had not expected anything humane from the SS. Still, this night, this silent, coldly cruel night began to overwhelm me even more than the sporadic reminiscences of the interrogations by the German Secret Police, called the *Gestapo*.

The stillness around me, the menacing silence, broken only by the quiet commands of the SS-Block-Leaders to the corpse-collecting teams, or their short laughs when dispatching the dying men, was particularly filled with doom and began to instill a feeling of despair.

I had already gone beyond the fear, terror, or panic—I had already learned how to deal with such feelings, and had developed resistance to them. I knew how to suppress fear, how to become immune to terror, and how not to succumb to panic. During the past long months as a prisoner, I had leaned how to stay alive among the dying or the randomly executed men. I had learned to manage the remaining resources of my body most efficiently, without appearing to be slow in carrying out the assigned heavy physical labor. I was firmly committed in my mind to be one of the last men to die, and I intended to live sufficiently long for the arrival of the first opportunity to fight back.

This night, however, began to drain my last resources. The seconds were too long, there were too many seconds in an hour The night itself had already lasted too long. Hunger still did not bother me. True, from time to time some thoughts related to food crossed my mind. These thoughts, however, were associated with the feeling of warmth and strength provided by food, and nothing more. Strength and warmth were necessary to stay alive, so food was desirable. The feeling of hunger was a useful indicator of decreasing strength, but since in these circumstances this feeling was distracting me from the ultimate goal of staying alive, this feeling had to be suppressed.

In addition, I had some bad luck. Being 180 centimeters [about six feet] tall, I was standing in the fifth and last row of my column, my back directly exposed to the frigid air. Worse yet, my back was also exposed to the efficient inspection of the SS-Block-Leaders, who were looking for the slightest breach of discipline, such as a turn of the head or a movement of the hand, to execute a swift and deadly punishment.

It was even too dangerous to glance at the reason for the punishment: the burned-out structure in the first circle of barracks, behind my back. To exchange a word with one of my neighbors in my row, to the left or to the right, could be fatal. All that I could do without any risk was to look at the clock above the machine guns, or to move my eyes slowly to the right or to the left, and to think—thinking could not be noticed if one was able to control his face, and this we had already learned. I could also make plans for the future, which could be useful if I survived this night, so I did. Nonetheless, I was still able to perceive the strange, irrational beauty of this barbarous night. I had an unreal feeling that I was present at the *Appellplatz* in two capacities—as a captive participant and as an uninvolved witness. Quite odd.

Midnight came—incredibly slow—and went, and time stopped once again. It seemed that I was not the only one who was hoping that at midnight we would be allowed to go to our barracks, for as the hour passed many men gave up and began to die. Teams of corpse-bearers, each of two men, became very busy. Now, they had to run not only when returning from the mortuary to the *Appellplatz* without a load, but also when delivering the collected corpses to the mortuary. Still, running kept them warm and the corpses were not so heavy—thirty to fifty kilograms [65 to 110 pounds], no more.

WHERE WAS GOD?

The moment came when I noticed that my already low body temperature began to drop more rapidly. There was little that I could do about it at that time. The calisthenics I learned to use to keep from freezing were becoming less and less effective. These exercises, such as rotating the shoulder blades, required very little movement and could be used with little danger when no SS-Officers were nearby. At that time my weight was down from 75 to about 40 kilograms [165 to 90 pounds]. I had already burned off all the fat in my body, and depleted muscle tissues do not produce enough warmth. Also, at such a low temperature the clothing made of a thin hempen fabric without lining does not give much protection against the elements, but this was all that stood between my body and the frigid air. My condition, too, was aggravated by the fact that the past day had been very hard for me. I had again been attached to what was called the *Speer Kommando*. The talented Reichsminister, Albert Speer, knew very well how to organize efficiently a twelve-hour workday. This very evening the *Speer Kommando*, two-hundred men strong had brought back to the camp corpses of ten men who did not manage to survive the organizational abilities of the *Reichsminister.*

The weather changed after midnight. Thin, low clouds covered the sky, light snow began to fall, and gusts of wind swept across the *Appellplatz*. One of the gusts brought to us the smell of smoky, wet timber from the burned-out barracks; another brought from the crematorium the repulsive sweet smell of the burning human flesh. This peculiar blend of odors, the slowly falling tiny flakes of snow illuminated by the powerful searchlight beams, the thousands of grim, mute, immobile men dressed in striped clothes with numbers on their left breasts and right legs, the randomly scattered corpses of dead or dying men as they dropped to the ground, the teams of corpse bearers running to and fro, the elegantly dressed SS Block-Leaders and SS-Officers walking leisurely and alertly among the columns, the unearthly stillness broken from time to time by the quiet, sinister voices of the SS-Guards, the whole scene partially obscured by the fog-like falling snow—all this gave the *Appellplatz* a very strange eerie character.

At one o'clock in the morning I lost all hope that we would be allowed some rest in our barracks before reveille at five o'clock. Indeed, I was not sure any more that I would manage to stand on my feet until then. At the beginning of this long night I looked forward to the coming of the reveille, trusting that it would be the beginning of a normal workday, with a normal death rate; now it appeared that I was too optimistic. The reveille was too far away.

Looking for anything that could give me some strength, I tried to compare the condition of the men in my column, many of whom were friends of mine, with the condition of those in the columns nearby. I looked left and right, moving my eyes only and slowly, very slowly, slightly turning my head. As I expected, we seemed much better off than the others. Our column consisted, for the great part, of young and strong army reserve officers and privates; they were the soldiers of a beaten but not defeated army who decided not to go to the prisoners-of-war camps despite the death sentence imposed—in violation of the Geneva convention—upon officers who refused to follow the orders of the occupation authorities, but decided instead to get away to join their units abroad but were not successful and were captured by the Gestapo German Secret Police. The others were university and high school students, members of the intelligentsia, workers and peasants, all brought up in a closely knit society which cherished strength of character, independent thinking, and a sense of duty. All of them were highly patriotic; they were grimly committed to staying alive until the first opportunity arose to inflict any damage upon the despised enemy. Thus the rate of dying among those with whom I stood was not as severe as it was in the other columns.

In the columns that I could see I began to notice a significant change. During the first few hours of this night the dying men had mostly been dropping to the frozen earth before they were actually dead; once fallen, they died quietly or were quickly dispatched by the passing SS-Block-Leaders. Now, however, the men began to die on their feet. They were not less subdued about it, as they previously had been, and were dying quietly as before, but now many of them were already dead as they hit the ground.

On occasion, I believed that I saw a look of disappointment on the faces of some of the SS-Officers—they were robbed of the pleasure of killing a fallen man.

A memory of an almost forgotten discussion carried on in the sophisticated, relaxed, and a bit hedonistic atmosphere of a big city, and ridiculously out of place in these present circumstances, crossed my mind— is it truly important, in a skeptical and enlightened twentieth century, to put as much emphasis on the development of the character as on the development of intellectual level and moral principles? Now I had all the proof supporting the traditional value system of an old society, but very little chance to convey this knowledge to the people outside the Dead Zone surrounding the camp.

I looked again at the clock—it was one-thirty. This was already the longest such night in my life, but there was still no end to it.

Then, very suddenly, I got a very strong feeling that someone desperately wanted my attention. Quite involuntarily my eyes moved slowly to the left and stopped at the face of my neighbor in the row. His face was white; his eyes were opened wide, and he was looking at me with an intense expression on his face. I glanced at his serial number—he was a German, a political prisoner, and had been in the camp longer than I was by only a few months. I did not know him personally, nor did I know the reason for his imprisonment. He could be a Catholic or a Communist, a traditional German aristocrat or a Social Democrat, or simply a young man dissatisfied with the National-Socialist system, who expressed his opinion too openly. Certainly, he was not a Catholic priest because the clergymen were, in addition, subjected to a special psychological treatment, developed by the well-trained psychologists in one service of the Nazi secret police, and therefore were kept in separate Blocks.

As I fixed my eyes on his face, his expression started to slowly change to that of resignation. I whispered, without moving my lips, the words "don't"— *mach's nicht* but it was to no avail. He slowly closed his eyes and an expression of a surrender covered his face. Suddenly he collapsed, slightly backward, falling on his left side. A feeling of both pity and weakness overwhelmed me. He was not much older than I.

Shortly afterward I heard the relaxed, strong and confident steps of an SS-Officer moving in my direction. The steps stopped where my companion lay fallen. I could not see the face of the SS-Officer since I dared not look up; a glance at his face would mean a breach of discipline, and that could spell death, not only for me, but also for my neighbors. I could however, continue looking down. Within my field of vision was my fallen companion, and the SS-boots. The boots were elegant and very well kept—typical boots of an officer committed to order and cleanliness.

My companion lay still, apparently dead. After a few seconds I saw one of the SS-boots—I do not remember any longer whether it was the left or the right one—lifting from the ground. The officer kicked my fallen companion in the chest, aiming, as usual, at the heart. A standard, clean SS-kick.

As it turned out, my companion was still alive. He lifted his head slightly, sighed, and said in a weak, completely quiet voice three words: *"Lass' mich sterben"*—Let me die.

I could not turn my eyes away, even though I expected to witness what was a common fact of life in the camp and what I witnessed so many times before—murder of a fallen prisoner. To my surprise, I was wrong. This time it happened differently. When those words were spoken, the boot, which a moment before kicked the fallen prisoner, hung for a few seconds in the air, and then slowly but resolutely returned to the ground. No second kick.

I do not remember now how long I continued looking at the still head of my companion, with the expression of ultimate quietness on his face as he gazed toward the sky, and at two immobile boots of the SS-Officer. The time stopped once again—nothing was changing. The boots were firmly rooted to the ground The SS-Officer was apparently waiting for some unmistakable sign that my companion was dead, but showed no intention to accelerate his dying. After a long, long while I thought that I could hear a sigh exhaled by the SS-Officer. A sigh of relief! Or of compassion? Or simply of resignation? I did not know, but the boots moved away.

Then, I remember, a very powerful change occurred within my mind and my body. The feelings of pity and weakness were slowly but steadily replaced by the feelings of anger and strength. I became convinced that I and many of my friends and companions would survive this so-difficult-to-survive night. And not only this night, but also thousands of other such nights, until the final victory. Our victory. Our case was just. We shall win.

The behavior of this SS-Officer puzzled me. It was very atypical. He let a dying prisoner die an almost natural death instead of taking the pleasure of killing him himself. Evidently, he decided not to earn an additional holiday in Italy, or an accelerated promotion, or some of the other distinctions which were routinely awarded to those SS-Officers most efficient in murdering prisoners. An inconceivable thought developed in my mind. Was it possible that the SS were not so monolithically barbarian as they appeared? Was it possible that there were some human beings among the repugnant SS?

To this day I do not really understand why this particular SS-Officer acted as he did. Evidently he knew the life in camp very well, but he acted almost humanely. When I look back, I tend to assess his behavior to be far superior to that of many citizens of the towns of Sachsenhausen and Oranienburg near our camp [about 30 kilometers (20 miles) north of Berlin]. They also had been very well acquainted with the camp. Nevertheless, with some rare exceptions, they chose to pretend not to know what had been happening in the camp, and not to perceive the obtrusive smell of burned human flesh coming almost continuously from the camp crematorium. They were scared. This SS-Officer, however, seemed to be different. He made a decision on his own, which was not in line with the established routine. Perhaps he is still alive—I would like very much to meet him again, after so many years, and ask the simple question: "Why?" "Why did you act as a human being when your orders were to obey cruel decisions made by your superiors?"

As the night continued, I grew numb, more and more. Nothing, except only one thing, mattered any longer—the dragging seconds, the sharp frost, the numbness of my body were now of little consequence. The only thing that mattered was to stay alive during that night, and to stay alive as long as it was necessary to have the opportunity to fight back. Oh, I knew, as all of us knew, that a night like this was only one of the challenges which we had already experienced, and there would be many more to come. And come they did, and we met them. Many of us perished, but the final victory was ours. My unknown German friend did not die in vain, nor did those who died fighting in the underground camp Resistance die in vain.

However, I had to pay a price. My spirit was strong, but my body was pushed just below the limits where even the strongest will can no longer substitute for body strength. One week later I noticed that my body entered the category of prisoners who were called "Muselman" in the camp parlance. I forgot the origin of this word, but I will never forget those prisoners. I remember them as if I had seen them but yesterday. The "Muselmans" were the prisoners whose will to stay alive despite all circumstances was broken, and whose bodies were damaged beyond repair within the conditions of the camp. The break-down of the will was leading to the break-down of self-respect, and as a result the proud human beings were transformed into the begging, scavenging animals. At that stage everything was rapidly going down-hill—"Muselmans" were dying simply of exhaustion within a few weeks. Their bodies had no fat; their muscles were shrunk, and so were their internal organs; their movements were slow and visibly impaired, and their eyes appeared cloudy; they had no pride anymore. They simply were dying on their feet as automatons having discharged batteries, and their weight at the time of the death was usually below 40 kilograms [90 pounds]. My own will and self-respect were as strong as ever, but my body did not obey me any longer and was continuously deteriorating. I noticed that the situation was very bad when I could no longer sit on a bench without experiencing pain where my buttocks used to be, and when I could touch my spine from the front of my body. There was nothing that I could do. It was simply not possible to recover when performing heavy physical work under the hostile sky, meagerly clothed, on nine hundred calories per day.

A few days later a miracle occurred. The design office of an SS-corporation lost its Czech engineers and could not find a qualified prisoner in the camp because such prisoners had already been killed, probably by mistake. Apparently, I was the only one, and professionally the most eligible prisoner, but I was still not eligible because of my sentence which limited my work assignments to heavy, unskilled manual labor outside of any building. However, the economic kingdom of the SS had enormous power, so my ineligibility was waived and I was assigned to the *Baubüro Kommando*—the Design Office Column. Yes, it was a paradise—all the time in well-heated rooms, no killing, even no beating during working hours, no raised voices, addressing the prisoners by German *Sie*, which is roughly equivalent to the English "Mister," and so on. And the easy for me, even enjoyable, engineering tasks, some of them quite advanced. A paradise. Under such circumstances it was much easier to stay alive during the remaining twelve hours of the day. In addition, the prisoners working in Baubüro were considered valuable property of the SS-Corporation, the *Bauleitung der Waffen SS und Polizei*. As a result, my status in the camp suddenly jumped from the lowest status of a prisoner who was at the very bottom of the camp hierarchy and therefore could be beaten or killed with impunity by everybody in power, another prisoner or an SS-Guard, to an elevated status of a "Prominent" who was protected by the status of his *Kommando* and his personal *Beziehungen* or "connections." It was well known that it was very dangerous to beat or to kill a Prominent—the executioner risked his health and often his life. So, a miracle occurred.

Unfortunately, it was too late for me. My weight continued to decrease, and I estimated on the basis of my camp experience that I would stay alive for no longer than three weeks—my wasted body became the rapidly deteriorating body of a "Muselman," despite my unbroken spirit. The damage to my body was too substantial. But then, after about one week, my Baubüro colleague, Georg Saur, noticed it, and approached me. My future good friend, Georg Saur, saved my life and had done it without hurting my pride. But this is a separate story.

The other consequence of this long night, the tuberculosis of the lungs, took over one year to develop. And again a similar story occurred. The brave medical doctor Zawadzki from Cracow (I forgot his first name) saved me from the gas chamber which was the routine SS-medication for such illnesses—he simply assured the SS-doctor in charge that he would arrest my tuberculosis within three months, and agreed, in the case of his failure to do this, to go together with me to the gas chamber. The SS-doctor accepted the deal, and again, a miracle occurred—my tuberculosis became calcified. Remembering this occurrence I bitterly regret that I did not find time after my return to Poland to find doctor Zawadzki in Cracow to express my gratitude. However, at that time his action was one of many such actions in the camp. Simply, such a behavior was expected from the old political prisoners. It was considered a duty. Nothing heroic. A routine attitude which sometimes misfired and the men died, often very painfully.

Epilogue:

Well, all this happened many eventful years ago, but that night, that decisive night, is too strongly rooted in my memory ever to be forgotten. I celebrate each infrequent anniversary of that Friday whenever it falls on the thirteenth day of February. I spend that day and night near a fireplace, with an ample supply of wood and a bottle, or two, of good wine on hand. Remembering so well the cruel coldness of the *Appellplatz*, I enjoy the gentle warmth that radiates from the flickering flames, and I look through the large glass door at our flower garden covered with the deep, soft snow whose sparkle is as amiable and friendly during the day in the rays of the low winter sun as it is at the night in the soft light of our garden lamps.

How different are the warm flames of our fireplace—so different from the cold probing fingers of the searchlights on the *Appellplatz*. How different and inviting the snow looks. I cherish the return to my planet, and I think about the long, hard, and cruel battle against a pragmatic, inhuman, and dedicated enemy, the battle which we won. Despite all the odds, despite thousands of such happenings as that night, despite incredible losses of life, despite all the reasonable and logical arguments, we finally won. We won, and, when winning, we broke the spirit of the mighty SS. At the end of the war many of them realized that they had been misled. They had believed that they were chosen to sacrifice their ethical standards for the sake of the future of the German nation, that they even were heroes. At the end, they realized that they had acted like criminals.

A few weeks before the end of the war, I had a very interesting conversation with three young, well-mannered SS-Officers from the Baubüro. They approached me and said that they wanted me to know why they behaved as they had, and stated that now they realized they had been misled. I understood them and understood their personal tragedy, and I told them so, but I also reminded them that they had violated basic moral standards, betrayed honor, and participated in unspeakable crimes. As I remember, they understood me. Better late than never. This destruction of the spirit of the so-dedicated SS was our biggest victory.

Yet, there still exist too many *Appellplatzes* on our small, beautiful planet—the only planet that we have. Our battle was won, but not the war. Not yet. But we shall win.

chapter sixteen

DEATH MARCH
THE BITTER CHOICE

by Jerzy Tadeusz Pindera

Introduction

My story is about an event that occurred at the end of my long imprisonment about 30 kilometers [20 miles] north of Berlin in the *Konzentrationslager Sachsenhausen, Oranienburg bei Berlin,* officially abbreviated as KL Sachsenhausen and called KZ by the prisoners.

It is well known that war leaves mental scars. The scars caused by Gestapo jails and Nazi concentration camps are deep and remain painful even after more than half of century. After so many years I am still not able to tell whether my action—in fact, my inaction—was justified. Perhaps writing about this event will lessen my burden.

This event has haunted me almost every day for more than fifty years. I remember quite vividly what happened the afternoon of April 28, 1945, seven days after we left the camp and began what is now known as the *Todesmarsch.* More than six thousand prisoners were executed during that march. I remember looking at numerous corpses of men, women, and children lying along the highways, but one particular and a quite typical execution is burned deeply in my memory—an execution that I may have had the power to influence. I wonder whether my decision on that day was ethical.

I have no doubt that my decision was reasonable, pragmatic within the accepted value system, and caused by a proper sense of duty and obligation to my native country. But I have my doubts whether or not those overriding principles could obscure the simple fact that a man died in despair, who perhaps, but only perhaps, could have survived if I had made the appropriate decision within about ten seconds.

At that time those seconds were to me an eternity. I assessed that I had about a 30 percent chance to save his life and not to lose mine during the rescue. In the KZ we took such chances even when the probability of success was considerably lower. However, the situation was different at this particular time. Having resisted the most arduous hardships for five years and three months, I believed that I should return alive to Poland. I saw it as my duty to use my war experience to reduce the killing and suffering which we expected to be re-introduced in Poland, this time not by the fanatical Nazis but by the fanatical Communists guided by the fanatical NKVD, later called the KGB. I wasted a precious ten seconds trying to reach a decision, and as a result a young man died.

This is one of two events that have haunted me since the Death March. The second event concerned my escape. I organized an escape two days later, early on the morning of April 30, 1945. The most difficult task was to blend among the population until we could reach a forest a few hundred meters [about a half a mile] away. Afterward, for more than twenty-five years, night after night, I dreamed about this escape. Each time I remembered the particular tickling between the shoulder blades where I expected to be hit by bullets fired by the alerted SS-guards, and I remembered that I did not dare to accelerate my pace because this would have made me noticeable to the guards. For more than ten thousand nights I tried desperately to wake up to end that dream. Fortunately, in recent years that dream has not returned.

However, the memory of that young prisoner stays with me, and stays, and stays, day after day. It stays with me in spite of the fact that I was already hardened at that time. I was an old prisoner, number 28862. By the time prisoners were given numbers higher than 144000, I had seen many thousands of prisoners die in the KZ. Many of them were my friends, and I remember them vividly and sadly. I remember particularly Janek Czapski, who died in my arms. However, that memory does not disturb my peace of mind. But this particular death was different. A few more days, and the prisoners who managed to stay alive would be liberated. It was bitter to witness a possibly preventable death at the very end of that brutal war. I did nothing, and a young man died in despair before my eyes.

My Story

There was no doubt that the end of the Third Reich was near. During the nights we could hear clearly the thunder of the Soviet heavy artillery. During the days we watched the Soviet fighters chasing overpowered German planes.

At that time small changes were already occurring in the KZ. First went the Puff, as I remember. The sexual services offered by a small *Kommando* of female prisoners, who volunteered for this job, were terminated at that time. The term "to volunteer," although technically correct is very misleading. Those young women had to choose between immense suffering followed by a very unpleasant, brutal, and undignified death within a few months, and rendering of sexual services in quite pleasant surroundings with death delayed by months or years. Comfortable accommodation, sufficient food, and shelter from cold rain and snow could mean survival. The ten or fifteen women who rendered sexual services lived in near the KZ hospital in a special separate barracks colloquially named Puff. Of course, the *Nürnberger Rassengesetze* were strictly observed: no Jewish female prisoners, German females for Germans and Scandinavians, et cetera. The SS authorities decided that moral standards must be upheld so no prostitutes were accepted. The work was not heavy: about eight clients per day, during four hours in the afternoon. Very few political prisoners used the services of those girls despite a quite low entrance fee of 2 RM paid to the SS officer in charge, but the majority of criminal prisoners had no such ethical constraints. There was a rumor that the women would be executed and the Puff destroyed, but it was too late to save them. The youngest were girls sixteen years old.

At about the same time, another particular *Kommando* was terminated. It was a highly classified *Kommando* consisting of professionally outstanding prisoners, mostly Jewish, accommodated in special barracks. The barracks was soundproof, made of brick, with a kind of air conditioning. The structure was located inside a cage made of heavy steel wire with very small openings. Prisoners in this *Kommando* received a double amount of food, meat every day, and excellent health service by KZ standards. The only task assigned to them was to make counterfeit copies of some documents and currencies of England, America, and France. Because of the sensitivity of such work, this barracks was isolated and operated discreetly; the disappearance of its inhabitants was not immediately noticed.

The atmosphere in the KZ became very tense. The *Reichssicherheitshauptamt* had already seriously considered the execution of all Communists and perhaps of some Social Democrats. To our understanding, the limiting factor was the capacity of the crematorium's four furnaces. The last reliable news that we received, on April 16, was that the Soviet Red Army had just crossed the river Oder, was moving in the direction of Berlin, and was crushing German resistance between the Oder and Berlin. We had been receiving information about the outside world from prisoners who were performing janitorial services in the offices of the *Inspektion der Konzentrationslager* located in Oranienburg [about 5 kilometers (3 miles) south of Sachsenhausen]. When the janitorial services rendered by prisoners in the offices of the SS administration were stopped, so also ended our reliable information.

What made this matter worse was that we could no longer learn about the plans made by the *Reichssicherheitshauptamt* regarding our destiny. We knew that the decision made by Himmler to execute not only the Communists but all the prisoners in the German concentration camps was rescinded because of technical reasons, but we could no longer gather reliable information. Unconfirmed gossip circulated that we were supposed to go by foot to the harbor Lübeck [about 250 kilometers (150 miles) northwest], be put in barges, and sunk. As far as I could learn, there were no plans to let us survive the end of the war. So we, the old prisoners, were tense. Amazingly, the young prisoners who were brought to the camp during the last year or so did not realize how serious the situation was. They firmly believed that the end of the war meant liberation and were not able to anticipate what would happen between Sachsenchausen and Lübeck during our expected long march. They could not believe that the terror killing of 1940–1943 could return. We therefore expected that many younger prisoners would die during the evacuation of the KZ. The reality was even worse than our expectations.

The refugee prisoners brought to KZ Sachsenhausen from other concentration camps, including men from Auschwitz and women from Birkenau, were telling the same story that we suspected: either you keep the pace with the evacuation column or you are shot. That pertained to all prisoners: men, women, and children. Because of the arrival of prisoners from the other concentration camps, the number of prisoners grew rapidly—from about 20,000 to more than 36,000 in April 1945.

Fortunately, at that time the prisoners' internal self-government was in the hands of Communists supported by Social Democrats. The criminal prisoners, so-called Professional Criminals or BV, would not be willing or able to dedicate sufficient effort to assure the necessary discipline, supply of food, medical services, or supply of medication stolen from the SS stockpiles. We already knew from experience that each time the BVs were in command of the KZ self-government the mortality rate increased rapidly, homosexual rapes and killings of prisoners by prisoners spread, and narcotics were brought to the KZ. So, in that respect we were lucky.

The great worry of the group leading the Resistance in the KZ was the unexpected arrival of women and the problems that this created. Women were accommodated in one of the barracks in the first row, and their very presence stimulated the imagination of women-hungry prisoners. We had to introduce strict internal rules because we could not afford any disturbance that could be used by the KZ authorities as a pretext to start a bloodbath. The situation was very tense, and we carefully avoided any action which could be considered a political provocation by the KZ administration.

At that time our discipline broke only once. It occurred outside the main concentration camp in the building of the *Bauleitung der Waffen-SS und Polizei*, where the *Kommando Baubüro* was working. Early in the afternoon the air attack alarm sounded, and we could hear the roar of bombs bursting close to us. The SS-Guards hid in the air defense shelter. Ignoring the order, we climbed on the roof of the building to look at the town of Oranienburg under a bomb attack. We felt invulnerable. I remember looking at a house close to us beneath which a heavy bomb exploded. The whole house was lifted in the air for about 100 meters [110 yards], and then it disintegrated in the air. We felt no pity. The inhabitants of Oranienburg knew well what was happening in the KZ, but the majority ignored it. The sweetish smell of burning human flesh is so distinct that nobody could be mistaken, and that smell very often penetrated into Oranienburg.

Fortunately our behavior was overlooked for two reasons. First, we were a so-called *Prominenten Kommando*, having various unwritten privileges, so the SS-Guards were not eager to report us. Second, and more important, our boss, *SS-Obersturmführer* (Fach) Josef Schnöll was in some respects an honorable man. He would never do such a thing as report us. His attitude and behavior were exceptional. So we had our short diversion before returning to the main KZ.

Because I did not know what the evacuation procedure would be, whether or not we would be searched when passing the main entrance gate, I did not arrange for any food supplies. All I could safely arrange was to gather some medication which might be needed during a long march to Lübeck. I had secured suitable clothing. When we learned during the previous winter that the probability of evacuation of KZ Sachsenchausen toward Bavaria was very high, I took precautions. At first I organized (in KZ parlance, the word "to organize" meant to acquire without money) a pair of strong, comfortable shoes, using the services of a prisoner working in the *Kommando* at the Crematorium, which operated a building called Kanada. Other prisoners, also with access to Kanada, brought me civilian clothes, workman style, dark blue. I could wear them safely, provided that the pants and jacket were marked according to KZ dress code. At that time typical clothing of KZ prisoners, the thin denim garb made of gray hemp with blue vertical stripes, was in short supply, so the KZ administration had to use the clothing of persons who were brought from the outside directly to the KZ Crematorium. The *Kommando* working in Kanada was in charge of cleaning and repairing the property of persons coming from the outside, who were executed and cremated in the furnaces.

My only problems were the marks on the pants and jacket. Red stripes, five centimeters [two inches] wide, were painted along both legs of the pants, a red cross was painted on the back of the jacket, and a red square was attached to the back of the jacket, above the red cross. The stripes and cross were of oil paint. Anticipating that escape from transportation would be necessary, I replaced the oil-painted stripes and cross by stripes and cross painted with water-soluble paint, which was easy to wash out, and I made sure that the red square would be easy to remove. Also I made a small bag, which hung from my neck, for my notebook, letters received during those long years, a small pocket knife, some needles and thread, and addresses of closest friends. I put a spare shirt, briefs, and socks in a small shoulder bag and added shaving tool, toothbrush, toothpaste, and soap. A small canvas-covered canteen and a thin cotton blanket over my arm completed my equipment. I was ready.

On April 20, 1945, we were ordered to stay in the main KZ. There were no roll-calls for the first time since I crossed the main gate of the KZ Sachsenchausen in 1940. No SS officers entered the KZ. However, the watchtowers with heavy machine guns were manned by the SS as before. We were informed that the next day the KZ would be evacuated. All prisoners—men, women, and children—able to move on foot were to leave the KZ in columns of five-hundred. Sick prisoners were allowed to stay in the KZ hospitals. No provisions would be available to transport weak prisoners. Prisoners would either keep step with the column or they would be shot. Now we clearly knew what to expect. Ironically, April 20 was Hitler's birthday.

My physical condition was satisfactory. I was 180 centimeters [about 6 feet] tall. My weight recovered during the last three years from about 40 kilograms [90 pounds] to about 65 kilograms [145 pounds], about 15 kilograms [35 pounds] less than I weighed in my student days. I could no longer touch my spine from the front of my body. The tuberculosis that had put me on the list to the gas chamber was healed by Dr. Zakrzewski from Kraków. He arranged a typical KZ deal with the SS-Executive Physician. In the span of three months either my lungs would be healed or both of us would go to the gas chamber. The cure of Dr. Zakrzewski was successful, my diseased lungs healed, and we both survived. So my physical health was satisfactory. My psychological health was also good.

My Polish friends and I developed some strategic goals based on facts which we had learned from our German friends working as janitors in the *Inspektion der Konzentrationslager*. We knew about the attitude and goals of the Allies formulated in Yalta [two months earlier, in February 1945], and we knew the situation in Poland. Decisions made by the Allies already prescribed a specific development in Europe. Thus after our return to Poland, we would be too weak politically to influence the course of the political processes that were already decided. All that the returning Polish prisoners could do was to attempt to moderate the terror which we expected to be introduced by the new administration in Poland under command of the Red Army and NKVD. For us, the victory over Nazi Germany was not the end of the war.

We, the underground prisoners' organization, were trying to maintain order in the KZ, but it was difficult. There were no problems with the old prisoners. All of us had gone through hell and were not willing to jeopardize our chances to survive. One of the adages of political prisoners was "*Uns kann Mann biegen, nie brechen,*" "We could be bent but never broken." However, the younger prisoners were still not able to look to the future, control their emotions, and control their thirst for revenge.

On the morning of April 21, 1945, the evacuation began. There was no inspection at the main gate and we were free to join any column. The columns consisted of 500 prisoners arranged in 100 rows, five prisoners deep. As I recall, women's columns left the KZ first. Columns of men followed: first mostly Poles, the most numerous national group in KZ; then Germans, then Russians, Ukrainians, Lithuanians, Italians, Frenchmen, Belgians, Hollanders, Luxemburgers, Norwegians, Yugoslavians, Czechs, Slovaks, and Danes. Political prisoners did not mix. The political prisoners joined the columns which only reluctantly accepted BVs [criminal prisoners]. There were no problems with the Asocials or with Jews. Problems arose with two particular groups of prisoners: Jehovah's Witnesses and pederasts.

The Jehovah's Witnesses were highly respected by the prisoners. Their unconditional honesty and sincerity were acknowledged even by the SS. But Jehovah's Witnesses were dangerous because they could not tell a lie. The often fatal consequences of their forthrightness did not matter to them because to them death was just a gate to a wonderful future. It did matter, however, to a lot of prisoners who wanted to stay alive and whose life often depended on a judicious lie at a proper time.

Pederasts, because they could not control their urges, were despised in the KZ. Self-control was held in very high regard among grown, terror-hardened men. We polical prisoners did not despise pederasts as such. Generally, we felt compassion for them because of their deviation. They were brutally persecuted by the Nazis, and we firmly believed that an illness should be recognized as such, so the pederasts should be given help. But we also believed that pederasts should be able to control their sexual urges, as many thousands of men and women dedicated to celibacy have been doing for thousands of years.

When the food supply in KZ improved, all normal prisoners needed women, but we decided not to use the services of the girls in Puff because they were prisoners like ourselves. We decided to control our sexual needs, but only some pederasts were able to control themselves.

Many pederasts did not hesitate to use all available means—threats, beatings, brutal rapes, and narcotic drugs—to force underage prisoners to have sexual relations with them. Because of the behavior of some of their number, all the pederasts were so despised in the KZ that they usually removed their identifying pink triangles before they joined the evacuation columns.

On the other hand, prisoners belonging to the category denoted as "Asocial" and wearing black triangles were tolerated by the political prisoners. That category encompassed high-class safe crackers, money forgers, and pimps in executive positions mostly from the known red-light district of Hamburg. Interestingly, we never discussed that issue in the KZ. Presumably, the reason for such tolerance was the fact that the crimes committed by the Asocials were of non-violent variety committed against money-making public institutions rather than against individuals. The Asocials were thus tolerated also during the *Todesmarsch*.

Jews presented a very particular problem. In the eyes of the SS, they were at the bottom of the KZ community. Our impression was that the hateful attitude of the SS toward Jews was caused not only by the *Nationalsozialistische Rassegesetze,* which defined Jews as a lower race to be eliminated, but also by the SS feelings of intellectual inferiority. In general, Jews were at a much higher intellectual and cultural level than were the typical SS-officers. We attempted to help Jews to survive, but our means were very limited. Nevertheless, it was possible to create an atmosphere in the KZ that Jews deserved help. In this respect some criminal prisoners joined the political prisoners and accepted the risk involved. I remember an occurrence when a criminal prisoner risked his life defending a Jew. Only the most chauvinistic members of the very conservative Junkers group remained anti-Semitic, but they had little influence.

Anticipating some unpleasant surprises ordered by Himmler, the members of the underground Resistance dispersed among various columns. That increased our chances of surviving evacuation. I decided to wait until noon, when it would be clear that the prisoners leaving the KZ were not being executed outside the KZ.

This precaution was a mistake. The first columns received food packets sufficient for a few days. About one kilogram [two pounds] of bread and half a kilogram [one pound] of sausage or preserved meat were distributed among the prisoners leaving the KZ. When my column was leaving, sausage or other meat were no longer available, and we received only bread. Of course, that was welcomed, but our chances of staying alive decreased significantly. We had to expect that we would be moving for several days without any additional food, and the lack of high protein food such as sausage would be detrimental to our strength. The older prisoners divided their bread in five portions, to last for five days. We expected to spend the nights in barns, and in a barn one can often find some raw rye or raw wheat. Just in case, many prisoners carried small steel cans to boil the grains if the opportunity arose.

About noon my column went through the main gate, which bore the optimistic adage, *Arbeit machr frei*, "Work Leads to Freedom." Perhaps some SS psychologists meant it seriously, but to us it sounded ironic and derisive. Very few prisoners during the past five years left for freedom through that gate, but many crossed that gate to be executed and burnt in the Crematorium. Having crossed the gate, I checked the surroundings: no sign of preparations or facilities for mass execution. I relaxed.

The next several hours were uneventful. As expected, the younger prisoners, unwilling to control their hunger, ate a large part of their bread rations. It was impossible to stop them. Talking was strongly discouraged, and it would be madness to risk one's life trying to help prisoners who did not want to be helped. Those prisoners believed that they knew better how to manage food.

We spent the night in a barn. The night was warm and quiet. There was some straw in the barn. As always, I undressed for the night, hid my shoes, covered my body with all pieces of my clothing, and put my blanket on the top of it. I was quite warm, a bit hungry (not for the first time), and fell asleep. I already knew, from my army days and the time of my interrogations by the Gestapo, how important good sleep is.

However, the night was not pleasant to the many prisoners who ate excessively—that is, who ate more than 200 grams [one-half pound] of bread. Larger amounts of food taken at once caused diarrhea, and that was deadly. As result, many of the younger prisoners were ill in the morning. Several were unable to march and were shot. Our fatalities thus began.

The next day, April 22, 1945, was difficult and eventful. Many prisoners were not accustomed to long walking, their footwear was not adequate, and they had digestion problems. Fortunately, the SS officer in charge was not eager to exterminate his column completely, so every two or three hours he gave a ten-minute break. Usually he tried to make a break close to a village well so that we could quench our thirst, but no food was given to us. The weather was acceptable: no sun and no rain. Temperature was moderate, about 18 degrees Celsius [64 degrees Fahrenheit]. Our pace was also moderate, between three and four kilometers [about two miles] per hour. Thus marching was acceptable except for the corpses of shot male prisoners that appeared more and more often.

It was too early in the march for a psychological breakdown. Surrendering to that meant stepping out of the column, crossing the ditch on the right side of the highway, and waiting for a shot in the neck. Prisoners were still strong and still had enough to eat. The bread they were given could have lasted for at least three days unless they foolishly ate too much at a time and experienced diarrhea.

The second night was uneventful, but in our third day of the march the density of prisoners executed along the highway and village streets increased. It began in the morning with one corpse every few hundred meters [yards], but it grew rapidly in the evening to about one corpse every five meters [yards]. Evidently, many men ran out of food because they had not learned how to suppress the unpleasant feeling of an empty stomach. That still did not overly bother us. During the last five years we saw many thousands of prisoners dying or dead, so a few thousand corpses more made no real impression.

However, in the afternoon the first corpses of women prisoners appeared, and shortly afterwards the first corpses of children. That shocked us. Women carry life. Women are special. Women should never die at a ditch along a highway. Execution of women is obscene. Children also are special. Children are safe in villages and in big cities. Children are protected by everybody. To harm a child is to do damage to the social fabric. The execution of women and children always has been a crime not likely forgiven. But this crime was happening now and with more and more regularity.

As usual, no food was supplied—just water. However, we were allowed to gather kernels of rye and wheat. Using two flat stones, we ground them as finely as possible and cooked them in cans over small fires. This was not sophisticated nourishment, but it was healthy and satisfying. The third night was quiet. There was no trace of preparations to exterminate us. But the bodies of executed women made a telling impression. We became allergic to the killing.

The fourth day of the KZ evacuation was difficult for everybody. The food rationed out was almost gone. Thus the number of prisoners shot and dying in the highway ditches was increasing. I reserved a small piece of bread for the next day, the fifth day of our march, but I could not imagine how we were going to survive afterward. However, our SS-Commanding Officer decided to help us. He bought some potatoes from a farmer and distributed potatoes cooked in their skins among the prisoners. I received three potatoes, and that made me optimistic.

We felt alone and abandoned. Walking slowly but deliberately, surrounded by grim SS-Guards, we occasionally encountered hostile farmers as we passed through the villages along the way. Gray sky was above us and budding spring around us, but no help, no compassion, no friendliness. And still no trace of the American Army and of American or Royal Air Forces. The Allies, who had such an efficient intelligence network in Germany, appeared not to care. We were left alone, with a deadly, dedicated, brutal enemy. Corpses began to smell. Nobody wanted to help us stay alive.

So it seemed at least. However, we underestimated the bravery and the dedication of young Swedes supported and encouraged by the Swedish Government. The Swedish Government, using its own means, forced the Minister of the *Reichssicherheitshaupamt,* Heinrich Himmler, to allow several Swedish ambulances to follow the columns of the prisoners, collect the prisoners unable to march but still alive, and distribute food packets to prisoners still marching. Evidently, Himmler was convinced that the SS-Guards, consisting mostly of the ruthless, death-hardened, torture-experienced *SS-Totenkopfverbände*, would be able to prevent the Swedes from coming close to dying prisoners and saving them. Fortunately, Himmler was mistaken. I did not see the Swedes at close range, but my friends saw them. Despite the threats of the SS Guards, Swedish ambulances were driven just at the end of the columns. The young, superbly trained Swedes were ready to jump with a stretcher within a second. Riding high, they could oversee the whole column, which was about 100 meters [110 yards] long. When Swedes noticed a prisoner leaving his place in the column, they jumped with a stretcher and ran as fast as they could to reach the prisoner before the SS-Guard could shoot. The Swedes were mostly successful.

In the evenings the Swedish ambulances would come close to the SS-Guard lines of various selected columns. A Swede in charge would seek permission from the SS-Commanding Officer to distribute food packages among the prisoners. My column was not so lucky before I escaped, but the fact that there was someone in the whole world who cared about us and tried to save our lives raised our spirits enormously.

Still no American or British planes appeared, and no help was rendered by the Western Allies. We understood that the Soviet Air Force was engaged in very heavy fighting around Berlin, but even Goebbels reported in *Völkischer Beobachter* that the Western Allies had gained air superiority over Germany. Why had no Allied planes appeared when their intelligence service was so good? Were we expendable to the Western Allies?

A few days later, about one week after the beginning of the KZ evacuation, disaster struck twice. For several days we were practically without food. A typical KZ portion amounted to about 1000 calories per day. Now we were getting much less, so we became hungrier and weaker. In addition, during the day we did not make any break for a long time, and the prisoners carrying canteens had very little water left. All the prisoners were very thirsty. I knew that my thinking and understanding were diminishing. I still had sufficient reserves of strength, but I felt that they were fast becoming severely depleted.

The first event was quite innocent. Sometime before noon I felt somebody touch my left arm and softly say, "water." My first impulse was to unhook my canteen and share my water with my fellow prisoner who was so inexperienced as not to carry some himself. But I wanted to be sure that this was an inexperienced prisoner. I looked and I was shocked. He was difficult to recognize because he had changed, but he was very well known to me, as he was well known to everybody in the KZ. It was Kokosinski. Kokosinski joined my column and was marching in the same row as I. Kokosinski, who had good connections with the SS and the Police, and could be equipped for evacuation as no one of us could. Kokosinski, who during the past several months was an uncrowned king of the KZ because of his open collaboration with the *Sonderkommission* of the SS and Police. Kokosinski, who had the reputation of a prisoner who caused the deaths of many of his fellow prisoners. Kokosinski, who was the last among those who deserved help. Kokosinski. I was stunned. Now, Kokosinski wanted water from me, and I strongly suspected that this was only a pretext to start a conversation with me. I ignored his request.

Now, many years later, my feelings are more ambivalent. On one hand, I should have given him my water. I broke the main KZ rule: always help your fellow prisoner, even if that would endanger your life. On the other hand, if the conversation sought by him would be noticed by other prisoners and he would be recognized, he would not survive the coming night. Too many men remembered his evil deeds. While all that is true, I still feel some shame.

The second event was disastrous. Emotionally, I was exhausted. Too many corpses of prisoners, especially those of women and children, lined the highway. Cruelly executed, they had died in terror. My feelings were at the edge.

Physically, I was tired but still watchful, which as I had learned during my past five years was so necessary to stay alive. I was scanning the rows of men before me and the location of the SS-Guards along the column, just in case. So I noticed a man immediately when he started to move out of his place, to the right side of the highway. He was marching in the middle place of a row of five prisoners, about twenty rows before my row in the column. My column, as other columns, had consisted of 100 rows, that is of 500 prisoners, eight days ago when we left the gate of the *Konzentrationslager Sachsenhausen*, Oranienburg near Berlin. It was still five hundred men strong because loses were compensated by prisoners from the decimated columns. My place in my row was at the right side, so my field of vision was excellent.

He crossed the ditch along the highway, sat down on the edge of the ditch, took a small piece of bread from his pocket, and began eating it. He was clearly waiting to be executed by the infamous *Genickschuss*, a shot from behind at the place between the spine and the head. As I remember, he was about 160 centimeters [five feet three inches] tall and quite slim, so his weight was about 40 kilograms [90 pounds]. He was not more than nineteen years old. I could not see his prisoner's label containing his nationality and number, which would have allowed an estimate of the date of his imprisonment. He appeared be a Russian or a Ukrainian, newly arrived at the KZ. He seemed without connections and without influential friends who could prevent his desperate decision. Evidently, he broke down in despair.

Looking to the right and backwards, I saw an SS-Guard at a distance of about 20 meters [yards]. Alerted, already taking his gun from his shoulder, the SS-Guard was preparing to administer one more *Genickschuss*. We were tired, hungry, thirsty, and many of us were sick, so we were moving in small steps, about two steps per second. Thus I had about ten seconds to make my decision. It was difficult. Oh, yes, I made a number of difficult decisions during my five years and three months of imprisonment by the *Gestapo*. Those decisions were physically and emotionally very painful, but morally they were straightforward: either I win at the end or I die honorably. I did not have to choose between bad and worse.

This time it was different. Whatever I would do I would violate one of the basic moral principles. I could make four steps to the right, grab that young boy, put him on my back, and return to my place in the column. I could carry him for a few kilometers [a couple of miles] before I would have to make appropriate arrangements. But the SS-Guard was already alerted. He could panic and shoot both of us, which could trigger a general panic. Normally it would have been an acceptable risk to take. But at that time, a few days before the final defeat of the despised enemy, I had other moral and major obligations toward my country, which had been betrayed at Yalta by the short-sighted Allies. We were needed in the new Poland to moderate the terror anticipated from Stalin. Our staying alive was part of a major moral obligation toward our families and our country.

It was not possible to satisfy simultaneously both moral obligations: to immediately help a fellow human being and to contribute in the near future to national survival. I could not reach a decision to this moral dilemma. The seconds ticked away. We were moving forward slowly, step, after step, after step. After about ten seconds, I heard a shot, the clean sound of an infantry rifle. It was over. I had failed. The lack of a decision was itself a decision.

My decision not to make a decision to save the life of that boy was logical and reasonable as confirmed by later events. I was allowed to work in Poland for eighteen years before I was forced to go abroad. Nevertheless, the feeling of guilt has never left me.

However, this bitter experience was not all that happened that day. Several hours later, a similar event happened, but the circumstances were different. This time I acted resolutely, perhaps because I was ashamed of my over-intellectualized reasoning. This time it was not an unknown Russian boy who broke and surrendered in deep despair; it was an old prisoner, a scion of an old Polish noble family well known to me. He lost his physical strength, broke, and wanted to give up and die. Death for him was more acceptable than prolonged suffering. But he had no right to surrender. He had obligations to the rest of his family, which had survived a holocaust of the Polish upper class ordered by Hitler and efficiently organized by Himmler. He had obligations to his country because of the leading position of his family in Polish society. All means had to be acceptable to his friends to force him to stay alive. Fortunately, he had several friends around him, and I joined that small group. We applied the tested KZ method: to get a man so angry that he was ready to go to hell on broken legs to kill the devils. It took us a few minutes to set him in that state. We made him angry. To do that we had to use methods which no gentleman would use when dealing with another gentleman. Yes, we succeeded in convincing him, but all of us had his blood on our knuckles. It was painful to us to act in such a manner, but we had about five minutes to force him to change his mind and to continue marching. Fortunately, a hand-driven water pump was quite close, allowing us to clean him and ourselves. Our method was not honorable though we considered it ethically justified. The man survived.

A few days later, upon arriving in the village of Hallenbeck on April 30, 1945, we received confirmation that our goal was the city of Lübeck, where we would be put on barges, towed outside of the harbor, and sunk. According to the radio information, which we were able to learn before the evacuation of the KZ, the American Army should at that time have already crossed the river Elbe and approached the city of Pritzwalk, which was close to Hallenbeck. However, there was no indication that the American Army was approaching, so there seemed to be no power which could prevent Himmler from completing his objectives. It would be foolish to accept such a death. A lesser risk was to attempt an escape from the transport.

So, in the evening of April 30, 1945, I organized an escape. Early in the morning of May 1, I escaped with two friends, Stefan Patyna and Janusz Wellenger. Our escape was successful and we suffered no physical harm. As I remember, the next twenty-four hours could serve as a libretto for an opera, a particular blend of very tense moments just a hairbreadth from death, some grotesque life-saving actions, several subtle romantic moments, and a lot of embarrassment in our first encounter with women after so many brutal years.

One day later, I spent the whole day sitting in the sun and eating strawberry preserves from a small jar which I found in a food cellar, using a silver teaspoon which I took from the empty mansion. I did not dare to eat anything else, or more. It would be very dangerous. Sometimes food kills.

Two days later, in the morning, the Red Army arrived. Before noon on May 3, 1945, I drank good French brandy with two young officers of the Red Army in an old mansion of an aristocratic family in Hallenbeck. We celebrated the destruction of the despised racial National-Socialist system. The fighting war for me was over. I was free. But I knew that the political war was coming.

And the scars remained.

part three
BEYOND SURVIVAL

chapter seventeen
MY WAR YEARS

by Remkes Kooistra

> Anyone who said "Freedom"
> Put his life on the line
> And chose the fight
> Devoted to God and Country.

> — *Trouw,* 1940–1945[1]

I: May 10, 1940–May 1941

May 10, 1940. It's early morning and I'm asleep, not unusual for a student who often works into the wee hours of the night. This morning, long before the usual hour of waking, I become aware of a droning sound, like of a swarm of bees. Reluctantly I wake up; it's only 5:30 a.m. Annoyed, I turn under the blankets. But the droning sound persists, and I also begin to hear voices outside, disturbed voices, alarmed voices: "war," "Germans." "attack"....

So it had come after all. Like most of the people I knew, I had not expected it would happen. Of course, my country would remain neutral, just as it had during World War I. We knew many reasons why it would be in the best interest of Hitler's Germany for the Netherlands to remain neutral in World War II as well. Then again, what did we know about the Nazi-spirit, this obsession with human superpower? They had come.

Quickly I got dressed and joined the voices. With other students from my dormitory I walked toward the center of the city of Kampen, our seminary town. We looked up to find the source of the drone, planes obviously, but we couldn't spot any. We walked on, past the house of our favorite professor, Klaas Schilder. He had heard the droning too and was already standing in the doorway. He told us: "Friends, I see hard times ahead. The enemy is satanic. It's not Germany as much as the philosophy of Hitler's National Socialism." He knew. Only seven years earlier he had received his Doctor of Theology degree from the Erlangen University. There he had observed the growing influence of German National Socialism. On his return he had published a small study in which he tried to make the Dutch people aware of the pagan and barbaric ideology of the German Nazi party, represented in Holland by its counterpart, the NSB. In our seminary year lectures he had linked for us Fredrich W. Nietzsche, Georg W.F. Hegel, Alfred Rosenberg, and Adolf Hitler.[2]

The next day I biked to my parental home, avoiding major roads as much as I could. But even on country roads I met long columns of German soldiers transporting war supplies. Their plans were no secret: use the *Afsluitdijk*, the shortest route, to capture the western part of the Netherlands. But they would be stopped, so our badly informed optimism told us. Were our soldiers not courageous? Dutch people had a national history of resisting foreign domination: Spain in the sixteenth and seventeenth century, England in the seventeenth century, and France in the 19th century. If Spain, England and France failed to wipe us from the map, Germany would not either. We were heroes. Our soldiers were heroes.

Heroes or not, they did not stop the German advance at the *Afsluitdijk* or anywhere else. What European army could halt the *Blitzkrieg* in those early years? Moreover, our army had been weakened by the lack of financial support during the depression of the 1930s and by a strong pacifist movement after World War I. Bad news followed bad news. Queen

Wilhelmina fled the country for England. We felt betrayed, and it took time to accept that a queen in England could do more for winning the war than a imprisoned monarch like the Belgian King. Rotterdam was bombed indiscriminately. In five days it was all over: we surrendered.

For most Dutch people the routines of ordinary life took over after the capitulation on May 14, 1940, but normalcy was only skin deep. In September, I returned to the seminary for my final year. Disturbingly, the only professor absent was fiery critic Professor K. Schilder, confined to a cell in the Arnhem prison. Soon other disturbing events occurred, reminding us of the new and dangerous situation that had developed.

The best and most popular dentist in town was Dr. Polak. He had his clinic at his house, a patrician mansion located in prominent part of town, surrounded by the elite of the town: doctors, lawyers, seminary professors, and industrialists. One morning in the early fall, we heard the terrifying news that Dr. Polak had tried to commit suicide. He, his wife, and their beautiful seven-year-old daughter were found unconscious by the housekeeper. They were rushed to the hospital, where the parents were revived. The daughter died, however. Jewish Dr. Polak knew what was going to happen to his people, and his fear may have been the reason for not having more children. The Polaks had tried hard to move to the U. S., but without success. Now they had to live with the guilt of their dead child.

It was then that the Christian community of Kampen sprang into action. The dental office was closed and the Polaks disappeared. A devout Christian family cared for them for the rest of the occupation, for five long years.[3]

Soon after the occupation, the German authorities distributed two kinds of questionnaires for Dutch citizens to complete: one for Aryans and a different one for Jews. These forms proved to be their first tools of persecution. Many later regretted that they had so willingly helped the enemies. Dr. Jan Koopmans, another prominent member of our academic community, immediately understood the possible deadly impact of this census, and he began to organize a student resistance movement. Being one of the leaders of our student organization, I attended the initial meetings where we planned our resistance policies. We helped distribute more than 10,000 copies of a brochure written by Dr. Koopmans titled, "*Bijna te Laat*" ("Almost Too Late"). In it he pointed out that all who had signed the Aryan statement were to some extent accomplices in the persecution of the Jews, for by doing so they made it easier for the Germans to identify the Jews. In a prophetic cry, he told the Dutch people: "Don't be mistaken about the Jews] *zij gaan eruit en zij gaan eraan* [they have been put out; soon they will be put down]." He paid for his resistance with his life. Like the German theologian Dietrich Bonhoeffer, he was killed in 1945, near the end of the war. I count it a privilege to have known this brave and perceptive man.

II. May 1941–September 1942

In early summer 1941 I returned to my parents' home in the village of Veenhuizen[4] to prepare for my final examinations. One of my professor examiners was also in hiding by this time. I was instructed to go to the house of a pastor in Utrecht for the oral part of my examination. In that pastor's study I waited for my professor. After about three hours, the pastor told me to go home. After a few weeks, my written exegetical work came back in the mail with a letter informing me that I did not have to do the oral part. The professor had attached a note of explanation: "*ex ungue leonem*," which means "because of the claw one recognizes the lion." According to my professor, I knew enough Hebrew to become eligible for the examination of the Bachelor's Degree in Theology, and that would lead, I hoped, to a call to the ministry.

III. September 1942–December 1943

In September 1942 I began work as an unordained pastor in a small congregation that spanned two villages in rural Friesland in the northern part of the country. It did not take me long to become aware of a growing active resistance movement in the country. For instance, a clergyman tire-lessly traveled up and down the country to find and organize hiding places for Jews and others. He was known under the alias of *Frits de Zwerver* (Frits the Wanderer), and his organization was called the *Landelijke Organisatie* (L. O., People's Organization). During the course of the war, the L. O. took care of thousands of people in hiding. As people in hiding could not get their ration cards, the L. O., with the help of more militant resistance groups, raided many offices for ration cards to help the *onderduikers* (the common name for people in hiding). Such "stealing" was called "organizing" then.

Soon after my arrival, I was asked to bring a young Jewish man to his new hiding place some 150 kilometers [90 miles] away in the far edge of our next province. He was given a new non-Jewish name, a good bicycle and a new identity card. All Dutch citizens had to have one by now, and Jews had a big "J" printed on theirs. Happily, no SS-soldier or *Grüne Polizei* stopped us. We had interesting conversations and arrived safely at our destination. Mission accomplished, I then dropped in the next day on my fiancee, who lived not far away. She was happy to see me, but I had to invent a story to explain why I showed up so unexpectedly in the middle of the week.

"Were you fired?" she asked. Without giving away my mission, I as-sured her I was not.

For our Sunday School Christmas celebration I wanted to use a large meeting room in the local pub. *Voor Joden Verboden*, (Forbidden for Jews) said a compulsory sign on the door. "Is there still no place for Him in the inn?" I asked the inn keeper? He was a "good" man, anti-Nazi, pro democracy, pro Wilhelmina. ("Bad" in the war were all people who col-laborated with the Nazis.)

"Go ahead; turn the sign around," he responded. So in this inn where Jewish people were no longer welcome, the village children celebrated the birth of another Jewish boy, born some 2000 years ago, for whom there was no place in the inn then.

Conditions under occupation steadily got worse, with a stream of announcements about further restrictions and persecutions. How impatient we became, and how eager for an end to this horror. Rumors abounded.

"Have you heard...?"

"Did I tell you...?"

"The Germans have been defeated in Russia, defeated in Africa; soon we will all be free...."

"*Radio Oranje* said...." (*Radio Oranje* was the BBC broadcast to Holland out of England.)

Various underground newspapers were not as optimistic, warning us that we would face even harder times before we could celebrate our liberation, but many of us refused to believe these pessimistic messages.

Germany, fighting on many fronts, was running out of manpower for its war industry. In the spring of 1943, it was announced that all former POWs (after the capitulation in 1940, all of the Dutch soldiers became technically prisoners of war) which had been sent home in 1940, would have to report for possible work in Germany. The impact was felt everywhere. Since I had not been in the army, I had not been summoned. Many of the "good" ex-soldiers went in to hiding. A young farmer, father of three small children, wanted to go in hiding but was understandably worried about his family. My fiancee Janette happened to be visiting, and we decided that she would stay at the farmer's house for moral support and that the husband would disappear on the day he had to report. The two women spent an anxious night without much sleep.

Specific resistance also increased rapidly, promoted by political leaders, by labor organizations and especially by the churches. The Dutch people had awakened. Now they knew.

The majority of artists and physicians refused to join the compulsory professional organizations set up by the Nazis. Doctors covered the shingles on their office doors. A spontaneous nationwide strike erupted. Trains stopped, offices and factories remained closed, and farmers poured milk into ditches instead of supplying the Germans.

German reaction to this May 1943 strike was cruel and immediate.

In one small farming community 16 people were arrested and shot, among whom were the father and two sons of one family, and the father, two sons, and a son-in-law of another. One of the victims was a fourteen-year-old boy, another a young man from Amsterdam who had come to the country in order to escape the growing food shortages in cities. In spite of the resistance, more than 100,000 Dutch men were rounded up and sent to Germany as laborers.[5]

IV. December 1943–May 1945

Not all things change in war times. The baker still bakes bread as long as he has flour, and the farmer plows on. People get married, go to work, get sick and die. In December 1943 I was officially ordained and became the pastor of my first real congregation, Siegerswoude, also in Friesland. I married my sweetheart, and we took up residence in the parsonage after a honeymoon of only two days. With the help of Janette's farmer brothers, we were able to serve a rather festive meal. Parents, other relatives, and friends gave us what furniture they could spare in this time of scarcity. We began poor in possessions but happy in our love.

It was here during the May strike earlier in 1943 that sixteen people had been killed ruthlessly by angry German soldiers. I counseled many of the sorrowing people. I baptized a little baby born after the massacre; she never would see her father. Janette and I spent much time with people who were mourning and asking: "Why did this have to happen? Where was God that early morning in May?"

Soon our home became a temporary refuge for people intent to flee from the enemy or hunger. L. O. people provided food ration cards for those who couldn't get them because they were on the run. I was a member of a small and carefully chosen team that distributed those cards. We knew where the *onderduikers* were housed. We often met in the public school office. The principal of that school was not a Christian, as most of us were, yet he would say, "If you people want to pray before we start, please, go ahead." In helping the *onderduikers*, we, capitalists, communists, atheists, and Christians of various denominations all prayed, planned, and worked together in a new brotherhood. Wartime breaks down barriers, promotes solidarity and ecumenism.

For a time we lodged a young Jewish girl. We had instructed her to avoid the kitchen window, which could be seen by our neighbor lady. This neighbor "entertained" German soldiers, and we were not sure whether or not she would betray people who protected Jews. The Jewish girl was not very careful, and we were happy that a more secure place was found for her eventually.

Soon we had to stay indoors after dark. Our house was located on the highway. Several farmers lived behind us along dirt roads. Two cousins had the same name: Ritske. One was "good" and the other "bad." The "good" Ritske was was very active in the resistance movement, even providing secret shelter for armed resistance workers.

Despite the prohibition to be outside, I often walked at night through my garden and across fields for a visit with *onderduikers* at the farm of "good" Ritske. I encouraged them, reported on any progress from the front, and gave them some religious instruction. Being an *onderduiker* was extremely boring and required lots of self-control. *The Diary of Anne Frank* describes this situation well. I kept on telling them: "Have patience. The day of our liberation is coming, maybe sooner than you think."

Our village policeman, Vogelenzang[6] by name, was "good." In uniform he attended several of our illegal meetings. To the German authorities he had to show dependability, but as our co-worker he supported the resistance. Whenever a raid was coming, we were informed of that danger. I remember two raids.

One afternoon he told us that the enemy had planned a raid for that evening. About fifteen of us decided that we should hide on the farm of the "good" Ritske. After a warm October day heavy banks of mist hung above the grasslands. Knowing the way, in deep silence, we marched through the night.

Suddenly the front man stood still. He had spotted somebody. A German soldier? With a gun? Perhaps one of a whole group? Are we moving into a trap? We stood still, questions running through our minds. The fellow does not move, what are we to do? Finally the principal of our Christian school whispered: "Stay here, I'll go." He advanced with vigorous steps, and coming close to the silent, immobile figure, shouted: "Friend or foe, let me go!" Then he started laughing, and soon we all laughed. The "man" was a pole, a lonesome pole in the field.

Our policeman warned us another time about a raid planned to find Jews in hiding. It happened that we again had a Jewish girl in our house, which did not happen often. Our L. O. friends did not want us to lodge Jewish people in the parsonage for any length of time. Our house was chosen to function as transitional lodging. To complicate matters, a very scared parishioner came to our house just then, asking me immediately ("Do you hear, pastor? I say: 'Immediately.'") to find a place for the Jewish woman they had been protecting for some time.

I told him to bring her to me: "I'll see what I can do." We didn't have time to spare. The custodian of our simple, small church was a "good" man. In the attic above the balcony, De Jong had prepared an emergency hiding place, hidden now by loose boards. It took considerable effort to climb the ladder to this very small place prepared with mattresses and blankets. After dark we took the two Jewish women there and put up the ladder. The older one suffered from arthritis, but she too managed to climb up. When we took the ladder away, the two women were imprisoned in their unusual, uncomfortable hiding place. I prayed that they would not panic and yell. Fortunately, that night no German soldiers came. The birds woke our stowaways early in the morning. They were very happy to leave their high bedroom under the slates. Some time later, they told me that they had quarreled up there for quite a while. I commented that no one should quarrel in church, not even in the attic.

V. *Pake* and *Beppe* (Friesian for Grandpa and Grandma)

In the fall of 1944, some L. O. people contacted me. Could I help a German Jewish couple in their early sixties? Hiding German Jews was even more risky than hiding Dutch Jews. The man had been a lawyer in one of the major cities of Germany. After *Kristallnacht* (November 9 and 10, 1938), they had tried to escape to the United States but, like others, were unsuccessful and got stuck in the Netherlands. When hunger increased in the western part of the country, taking care of this couple in the Amsterdam area became more difficult, so they were brought to the village of Siegerswoude in Friesland. Their daughter Clemmie (for that was her name) stayed in the western part of the country; her Jewishness could easily be disguised.

Near Siegerswoude lived a young farmer. His house, like many in that area, had a *mooie kamer* (beautiful room), a salon for special occasions which also had one or two alcoves for overnight guests. He was willing to take the risk for himself and his family by providing lodging for this fugitive couple in that room. His three small children were not yet of school age, so there was little danger that the children would betray their "guests." Because the Jewish couple had the age and appearance of grand-parents, it was decided that the children would call them *Pake* and *Beppe*.

I visited that home every week, talking with the farmer family in their living room and with the guests in the *mooie kamer*.

As the raids for Jews became more frequent, our hosts became anx-ious. Arjen, the husband, had a terrible struggle with his conscience. He knew that it was his Christian duty to protect his Jewish guests, but he became more and more afraid for the safety and life of his wife and children. In the end, having trouble sleeping at nights, he decided to ask me to be relieved from his Christian duty. I promised to try to find other accommodations for the couple.

Along a dirt road, a mother and her bachelor son lived in a small house a considerable distance from the highway. Once more I took the risk of explaining everything. They agreed to host the couple. But how could we get them there? My friend Sip, a distant relative of my wife, was not easily frightened, and he also owned a sturdy bicycle. He was willing to help. Early morning would be the best time, with farmers busy in the barn and little chance of Germans in the neighborhood. At 6 a.m. we peddled, Sip with the man and I with the woman on the luggage carriers of our bikes. It was probably the first time in their lives that the couple had sat on such a small bicycle seat. It was a risky adventure. What if the enemy saw this unusual convoy? We said a silent prayer for God's protection and, happily, we met nobody on this trip.

At first everybody seemed happy. Communication, however, was difficult. The mother spoke mostly Friesian and the couple spoke only German. In this much smaller house the living quarters for the Jewish couple was much more cramped. On a warm evening in September they took a short stroll for some fresh air. Unfortunately, they were spotted by some neighbors who could not keep their mouths shut. The hosts felt they could not lie to their neighbors. Once more I was asked, "Would I find another place of hiding for them?"

As I wondered what to do next, I received help from an unexpected corner. My bachelor friend talked with his friend Jacob DeWal, who volunteered to take in the Jewish couple. His farm was located next to a bunker, the home for a detachment of German soldiers. Close to this bunker the sixteen people had been killed during the May strike. Jacob told me: "German soldiers come to my farm every day to buy extra milk and eggs. They will never suspect me of having Jews in hiding at my farm. It is the safest place in the country."

We told our German couple: "*Abjetzt verstehen sie kein Deutsch mehr. Sie sprechen nur Frieschisch.*" ("From now on you don't understand German any more. You speak only Friesian.") They did their best, I must say. While they lived in this farm's *mooie kamer,* the woman sometimes helped in the kitchen. But she would always stare past the soldiers when they asked something, as if she could not understand. She was an excellent actor. The children of the hospitable farmer and his wife liked their new *Pake* and *Beppe.*[7] The Jewish couple stayed at the DeWals till the liberation in May 1945. I always felt that Jacob DeWal should have been given a special reward after the war; he was a quiet hero, one of many.

After liberation the Jewish couple learned that their son, Claus, had escaped from a transport train and via France and Spain had made his way to Israel. Their daughter had found a hiding place with an excellent Dutch family in the western part of the Netherlands. She too survived. You can imagine the happy reunion. The son returned to Israel, and parents and daughter emigrated to California where they started a chicken farm. I admired their energy. For some years we received a Christmas card from them, Eduard and Marie Siemons, whom we had protected.

After the war Jacob DeWal was too restless to stay in The Netherlands. He and his family emigrated to Canada. On a vacation trip in the early 1960s my wife and I visited Algonquin Park with our four children and my parents, who were with us from the Netherlands for the very first time. We planned to camp along the river near the little town of Renfrew. However, the mosquitoes made us change our plans, and we decided to look for a motel instead. Then I remembered that Jacob lived somewhere in this area. Why not drop by and say hello? But who would know where he lived? A small truck approached us at great speed. We flagged the vehicle down and asked the driver, "Would you perhaps know where a certain Jacob DeWal is living?"

"I sure do, for I am Jacob myself!" came the answer. He invited us to his farm. "No, no," he and his wife said, "no need to look for a motel; our house is big enough." My parents were given the special guest room, another *mooie kamer*. The rest of us preferred to sleep in our tent on the lawn. Just like the Jewish couple during the war years, now we, freely traveling in Canada, enjoyed the generous hospitality of Jacob and his wife.

VI. My father's imprisonment

My father was one of seven nurses in a small hospital of a minimal security prison. All but one were strongly opposed to the Nazis. The exception was Mr. Esselbrugge. When he was around, the others clammed up. Esselbrugge was an opportunist who hoped that by helping the occupying authorities he could quickly be promoted. He had joined the Dutch Nazi party and we could not trust him.

The Germans knew that almost all people of our prison-village were intensely anti-Nazi. Toward the end of 1944, becoming aware that they were losing the war, the SS became more ferocious. They decided to exercise their remaining power to discourage any resistance. On one December morning about ten leading people of the prison community were arrested, my father being one of them. On his way to inject a patient, he was stopped by NSB policemen. He was searched and they found in his stockings a number of illegal *Trouw* newspapers that he always helped to distribute.[8] He was not allowed to go home or even use the telephone to inform my mother. Together with the other arrested local leaders, he was brought to a prison in the nearby city of Assen. When Janette and I heard about it, we immediately went home to comfort my mother. She was in tears and thought she would never see her husband again. I tried to think of ways of helping my father to escape.

The next day I went to the prison, hoping to see my father. I knew one of the guards, and he told me that my father was in good spirits. But when I asked him about a possible escape, he explained that if he let my father or any of the other political prisoners escape, the Germans would certainly react with reprisals. "As long as we can function here, we can help the 'good' prisoners somewhat. If we are gone, there will be nobody left in the prison system to help them."

I knew that underground attacks on prisons in Amsterdam and Leeuwarden had been successful. But after those, prisons had been made more secure, and it would have been irresponsible to risk additional resistance workers. Even though I did not like it, I had to accept what I was told.

My father did not stay long in that prison. After a few days he and the others were transported to a prison camp, a so-called work camp, in Wilhelmshafen, in northwest Germany.

The Germans were losing, however desperately they were fighting in the Ardennes forests around this Christmas time. They were running out of war materials, and they had lost supremacy in the air. Every night we heard hundreds of bombers flying over to attack strategic targets in Germany: factories, electricity power-stations and railroads. Many civilians died in these attacks. Often when I stood outside in the night looking east, I saw the rosy glow of the fires burning in Germany. On such nights I wondered: "Is Wilhelmshafen being hit also? Is my father still safe?"

My father returned just before the end of the war, in April 1945. In the camp, food had been scarce, the daily main course consisting of a watery cabbage soup served with a piece of dark-grey bread. After a few months all prisoners looked like walking skeletons. It seemed impossible that only a few months ago their clothes had fit. Many died.

My father never talked much about his camp life. But he told me once that he used to encourage especially the younger inmates when they were ready to give up and die: "Clench your teeth. Think about your wife and children. We will return!"

I particularly remember one story he told years later. "I worked with sick people in the barracks. One prisoner suffered from diphtheria. I agreed with the doctor that we had to operate immediately; otherwise the patient would die from suffocation. We could use only the kitchen table for the operation. The only knife available was a potato-peeling knife. This we cleaned as thoroughly as possible. There was not much time and we had to act quickly. We had no cotton-wool to stop the bleeding, only some greyish toilet paper. Nor did we have anesthetics. We put the knife to his neck to open up the bronchial tube beneath his throat. This brought immediate relief for this suffering man. He healed quickly without any infection. We thanked God for his recovery."

By April 1945 the end of the war was in sight. Many German officials wanted to remove all traces of the concentration camps. The civil and military authorities agreed to load all Wilhemshafen prisoners on an old ship, sail it up the North Sea, and then sink it with all of its "passengers." But the German doctor who had worked with my father in the camp protested. He persuaded the authorities to ship all the prisoners back to the Netherlands, which could easily be done because Wilhelmshafen and the eastern border of the Netherlands were separated by a bay only about ten kilometers [six miles] wide.

And so a few days later about seventy camp survivors went ashore in Delfzijl. They looked terrible, wearing the clothes in which they had been arrested and in which they now were almost drowning. Yet they were happy, free, and back in their own country. If they had been strong enough, they would gladly have kissed the Dutch soil. They were warmly welcomed by the Delfzijl people, who had not suffered the hunger that the people in the western part of the Netherlands had. The citizens of this farming area, filled with compassion, came with milk, bread, butter, and cheese. But my father, always a nurse, shouted to his comrades: "Be careful. I know you are hungry. I am too, but if you eat too much of this good stuff, you'll become very sick." Those who listened had very little trouble. Those who could not withstand the temptation became very ill, and some even died.

My father, a man of duty, did not go home immediately. First he made sure that the sick ones received nursing care as they were transported to their respective homes.

Having finished his task, he returned to his own home. My mother was happier than I can describe. She wept, but this time with tears of joy. I received a phone call informing me of the good news. Happily, my best friend, a blacksmith, still had some gasoline, and on his motorbike he brought me to my parental home, some 50 kilometers [30 miles] away. We were not yet liberated. Groups of soldiers on their way back to Germany, as soon as they imagined any provocation, sometimes shot innocent Dutch people. The roads were not yet safe, but my friend and I made it without much trouble. I entered our home, embraced my happy mother, and entered the living room to greet my father. There he was, but I hardly recognized him, so skinny, so old he looked. But his voice was still the same, his handshake too, though weaker than before. We spent an hour of deep happiness together. Then my father grew tired and needed to rest. It took him a whole year before he was able to return to his work in the hospital.

Notes

1 During war time the illegal paper *Trouw* (*Faithful*) was established. It served with two or three other illegal papers, printed on clandestine, often primitive machines in obscure cellars, to keep the Dutch people informed and to encourage the resistance spirit. After the war *Trouw* sent to its helpers and distributors a small plaque in appreciation. It contains the words I translated at the opening of this chapter. The Dutch text reads:

Wie "vrijheid" zei, schreef 't leven af, En koos de strijd, God en het land gewijd.

I have always treasured my plaque.

2 After the German invasion on May 10, 1940, Schilder wrote weekly articles to make us aware of what was really happening and the dangers ahead. It was especially his article *"De Schuilkelder uit, de Uniform aan,"* ("Get out of the Bombshelter, Put on Your Uniform") that helped many to wake up to the reality of the ideological warfare. Schilder himself became an early victim. The enemy also read the journal in which he wrote, *De Reformatie*, and arrested him, trying to silence his opposing and warning voice.

3 After the war he continued to attend worship services in a large Reformed church in Kampen. One time one of his former friends asked Dr. Polak whether he did not find it boring to attend services in that "old stuffy church."

He answered with a question: "Do you think we had much fun at the parties we used to have before the war?"

4 Veenhuizen was the location of a minimum security prison which became "home" for many homeless drunkards. The large prison had its own hospital where my father worked as a nurse.

5 Dr. Louis DeJong, the official historian of World War II in the Netherlands, reported that many of these laborers did not return to Germany after their "vacation." By April 1944 the number was down to 14,000. *Het Koninktrijk der Nederlanden in de Tweede Wereldoorlog*, vol. 7 ('s-Gravenhage: Martinus Nijhoff, 1969–88, p. 1032.

6 Vogelenzang translates to "bird's song," a very unusual name for a very unusual policeman.

7 Children played an important role in the resistance movement. It is remarkable how well they could keep secrets.

8 DeJong, vol. 7, p. 838, reports that in the beginning of 1941 some 57,000 copies of the underground resistance newspapers were distributed but that this number had increased to 450,000 by the end of 1943.

chapter eighteen
THE STAR

by Clara Asscher-Pinkhof

An earlier chapter in this book contains excerpts from Clara Asscher-Pinkhof's autobiography, Danseres Zonder Benen [Ballerina Without Legs]. *The following excerpt describes her internal struggle between obedience and integrity, her parental struggle between wanting to influence her son and wanting to encourage his independence. The passage dealing with the Jewish star[1] begins with a humble confession:*

Even at the time when deportations became more frequent, I felt a security rising within me: it is not important whether or not I die, but *who* I am when I die. A kind of firm steadfastness surrounded me as far as it concerned only myself. But when this fate began to touch my dearest loved ones, this steadfastness was not sufficient.

A short while after the star had become mandatory and a short while before the telephone was taken away from us, the young successor of Avraham phoned me from Groningen in desperation about what to do to persuade my son Jitschak. Jitschak wanted publicly to refuse wearing the star. He did not want to go in hiding—that possibility was not in focus yet—but he wanted to show to anybody that he was a man who wished to defy this kind of blackmail and had decided to do so.

The young rabbi anticipated the fatal consequences of this deed and wanted to obtain my help to prevent him from doing what would certainly become his destruction. He discussed this with me by telephone with all kinds of Hebrew words among the Dutch, yet clearly enough for me to understand. For as a matter of fact, I knew that Jitschak wished to stick to his pure principles, accepting their consequences whatever they might be.

A terrible anguish for my boy strangled me. I responded that the rabbi should entreat Jitschak in my name to give up this plan. I was going to write him myself. Only write him? Suddenly I felt the desire to have the boy here, with me, in order that I could talk with him as with a grown-up man. And just as quickly I also thought he might be able to talk with his friend Kurt, an artist who had returned from the U.S.A. for family reasons and had missed a last chance to escape to the New World. I realized I was just a woman. What did women know about the heroic decisions of a man? A man should confront my son—a strong personality, like Kurt. For the very first time I realized how the masculine emphasis in the education of my sons had been lacking. These thoughts went through me in just a second.

"Can Jitschak get a travel permit?" I asked the Rabbi, for without a travel permit Jews could not travel anymore.

"I think so," he responded. "Yes, I will try to do that for you."

There was something like relief in his voice; he was not carrying the responsibility all by himself anymore—the mother could perhaps accomplish what he had tried without success. But when I put down the telephone, that mother herself was suddenly very insecure. Did I have *the right* to keep him from doing what to him was a spiritual necessity, even if it would cost him his life? And if he would be allowed to live on because he had surrendered to the ruling supremacy—how could he be able to live on as if nothing had happened? Was I not the maternal animal which just protected the body of her young ones? I did not know it anymore. I really did not know it anymore.

Jitschak came home, wearing the star. He told me, quietly and friendly, that he had decided to do this for my sake, but that it had taken away from him something very precious.

I had forgotten how much he had become an adult, a man.

Note

1 This chapter is Remkes Kooistra's translation of Clara Asscher-Pinkhof's *Danseres Zonder Benen*, (17th edition; 's-Gravenhage: Leopold U.M., 1984), pp. 141-142.

chapter nineteen
THE WESTERBORK TRAIN
STORY OF A COLLABORATOR

by Jacob Presser

Dr. Jacob (Jacques) Presser, former professor in the department of Modern History at the University of Amsterdam, is best known as the author of Destruction of the Dutch Jews, *the history of Dutch Jews during World War II. In 1957, Presser wrote a novella titled* De Nacht der Girondijnen *(The Night of the Girondists), a title intended to hide the real content of the book. Referring to the most bloody episode of the French revolution, it presented a moving parallel within the Holocaust of World War II.*

I obtained permission from publisher J. M. Meulenhoff, Amsterdam, to translate a few pages from this novella,[1] a section about the Westerbork Train. That section tells the story of Jacques Henriques, a Jewish history professor deported to Westerbork, where he collaborated with the Nazis to save his own skin. Though he became adjutant to the chief of staff serving the SS camp commandant, he saw himself not as a hero but as a traitor to his people.

The train. The train. It comes and it goes, but even more intolerable than its arrival and its departure is the regularity in which these take place. It may be storming, snowing, or freezing: the train goes. No sirens warning of an aircraft attack stop the train: it goes. Allies may destroy entire

193

railway junctions, they may demolish bridges and hangars, workshops and materiel, but the train goes. In Amsterdam there was once a strike because of the deportation of a few hundred Jews, but here in Westerbork[2] the train transports thousands of Jews away without any interruption. Everyone does his duty and nobody refuses; not a single sleeper is disturbed and not any nut is loosened.

The train is the devil. As it looms up out of the darkness with its dully glaring headlights, as it yells out its triumph over us with its piercing whistle, as it slowly, dashing and thumping, slides alongside the platform and finally comes to a stop with its hot hissing and trembling reverberation, it looks like a prehistoric animal of tremendous power, like the dragon from an evil myth. Suddenly it is standing there in the middle of the camp as if it had been conjured up from hell by a magic formula. In one respect Georg[3] was certainly right: compared to this train, the guillotine is a toy.

And then remember that it appears only in the fourth and fifth acts— acts of the tragedy that plays here once a week—a drama that is always the same and yet different each time. But the moment the demon comes thundering up from the abyss, everyone feels its presence, as inescapable as the thundering trumpets of the Last Judgment.

The drama starts Sunday afternoon. Act one presents the phenomenon which Cohn[4] once accurately characterized as the projector of rumors turned around one-hundred-and-eighty degrees. During the entire week this projector is directed towards the outside world, especially on the war facts. It tells us which cities have been taken back from the Nazis, what Churchill is planning to do, and how deep Mussolini is stuck in dirt and muck. Stopping to think a bit more about this now, I conclude that the rumor projector does not tell any lies. What it says is truth, but only future truth. It states though it ought to prophesy. The cities it mentions will indeed be taken back, but not yet, much later and for many, if not for all of us, too late. But here it is the same as at school: we just want to believe the good news, we want to enjoy the short daydream, we want to rock ourselves to and fro in the illusion. But on Sunday afternoon this projector turns toward the inside, toward ourselves, toward the next few days and hours, and it becomes annoyingly inaccurate. "The train will not come," but it always comes. "Schaufinger isn't here." Wrong again. Schaufinger is nearly always present. The only time he was away on vacation, Frau Wirth did the job even more cold-bloodedly than he. Another rumor: "We will be exchanged." But Jews are apparently either too costly or too worthless to be exchanged for anything whatsoever in the world. "The government in London[5] must.... Sweden may.... Stalin will.... Roosevelt can... Churchill shall...." From all these certain happenings at least one thing follows for sure: "This week there will be no transport, no train." But still the train comes; of course it comes. It always comes. The clock may stand still, but the train comes.

Every week, on Monday afternoon, there is a meeting at Schaufinger's place. The rule requires all to be clean shaven, to have polished boots, and every button in place as for a solemn ceremony. And so it is. Sometimes I played with the blasphemous idea that the meeting should be opened with prayer.

The round table is ready for the session, a session of the Council of blood,[6] as Jacob[7] says. The Camp Commandant is the only one without a star, just like Napoleon without any decoration in the midst of the gold-braided uniforms of his marshals, he being the only man with authority.

How many? That is the crucial number. The number is like the 666 in the *Revelation of John*; the number appears, the number rules, the number *is*. The number is the number of the beast. We know very well where it comes from, and we realize that we can no more change it than the reading of the barometer. A mathematical number may be composed of various factors, but this, this camp number, consists of human beings, one by one, counted together: all kinds of people, very different from each other, men and women, older ones and younger ones, but now united and separated from all the others, all one trembling mass. Each number— I cannot repeat this often enough—represents a human being, part of our humanity. Here they are in anguish, in death agony, and rightly so.

We are going to count. Cohn has his notebook ready and unscrews his fountain pen. First are those who have not been assigned to a regular barracks, the pariahs in this strictly caste-structured community. All those who have been assigned to the penalty barracks and those in the lepers hospital are taken. If we are lucky, those will make the number for this week. If..., but it does not always succeed. We *must* assemble enough people for the work camps, so we must find more people in all nooks and crannies of the camp. Especially the sick ones have a good chance to be selected. It seems that the sick must be particularly suitable for work camps— the sicker you are, the easier you qualify for transport. But if even then we do not reach the number, then we are heading for disaster. Nothing helps any more. Suddenly all the thousands of little dikes by which people tried to protect themselves, sometimes by paying bribes of thousands of guilders, burst. Imagined safety is lost. Rubber stamps prove invalid. Identification documents are scrap paper.

Yes, the number gives us headaches, but we make it, we always make it. And in the end we don't care too much, for we *Dienstleiters* (heads) can stay. Our names are written on the "list-of-ourselves."

The camp is waiting. They don't know anything, but the number leaks through, heaven knows how. Once again nobody knows anything, but they suspect.

O night of all nights. In vain I try to imagine how I lived through them, but I don't succeed. If I could, I might fall down as one dead. O night of vengeance, the night of judgment. In my barracks I often had to read the list, and I remember how the first names sounded in the silence—the chaos before the creation cannot have been more silent. It was as if the deaf listened to me, as if the blind looked at me, all of them frozen in extreme motionlessness. The list was in alphabetical order, but nobody trusted it entirely. Only when I finished the reading did the pandemonium break loose. I have seen people dancing, wild with joy, as if they were whirled around by an elementary power, kissing each other and touching each other obscenely. Others were running around as if they were out of their mind. They would fall down and stand up again repeatedly, they would bump against the benches, against the tables, against the wall, till finally they would remain lying on the floor, kicking and beating.

I have seen a woman who bit her sister, who was not selected but spared, in her jugular vein. I have seen a man cut out his eyes right in front of me while only three steps away from me another one was sobbing with joy. I have seen all this, I myself, many nights of doom. *I have seen all this.*

The fifth act is played in the early morning. The condemned have packed their belongings. They were helped by other happier barracks people, and they were supplied with liberal gifts. People would write each other, would think about each other, would bring greetings to those who had departed earlier. "If you see Rika there..." They would always say "there." never Auschwitz. This word was never mentioned. People who usually were terribly moody, rigorous egoists suddenly became good Samaritans, if only for a few hours.

Then the procession prepares to leave for the train. With all those backbags it makes for a lugubrious exodus, our own *Beggar's Opera*. On the platform stands Schaufinger with Bubi.[8] Up to the last moment Schaufinger remains approachable. Couriers come in the nick of time from Amsterdam. He reads the requests, very attentively, for he knows his duty. Bubi sometimes distracts him and then one of these requests may blow away. That happened recently, and when I wanted to get it for him, he signaled me not to worry about it. He is absolute tranquillity. Stiffly he stands as the procession passes in front of him: *morituri eum salutant.*[9] Let me make a confession at this time: actually he is better than we, we Jewish collaborators. For we have only one wish, that the train will take off. We wish that this will be over so we can return to our heated offices and again light a cigarette, for we are not allowed to smoke here. We feel a bit of resentment for these unlucky ones, who in their cattle boxcars hold on to every minute they can stay longer, hoping for the miracle that never occurs.

And when the train finally moves away, we return to the office, as with a funeral, chilled to the bone but relieved, with the irresistible need for a cup of coffee, which we detest as we drink it. And in the barracks people are fighting again, this time about the distribution of the poor belongings left behind by those who have departed.

One more episode I have to mention. We had a rabbi in our camp, Jeremiah Hirsch. He became my downfall. This is how it happened. I knew for a whole week that the rabbi and his whole family would be on the train list. I had tried to persuade my supervisor, Jacob Cohn, to save the rebbe.[10] But I had failed; Cohn proved completely intractable. He began chaffing me a bit and asked how I had enjoyed Leah, the plucky Jewish mama who was in Hut 16 with the twins. And when I indignantly denied this, he preached me a little sermon on the familiar subjects of hardness, blind obedience, and a bit more emphasis on the danger that threatened me if I did not obey his commandments.

Then he informed me that according to rumor the "rabbi" and the Jews in the next transport were not to go to Auschwitz but to a camp Sobibor,[11] which must be some sort of "extermination camp." I was inclined to regard the whole affair as idle chatter of intimidation. If the Germans want to exterminate us, why not here? Why are they using an enormous mass of people and equipment for these trains when they so desperately need every soldier and every car?

In any case, Cohn would not do anything. That night, a week ago today, I had to read the list in barracks 57, and his name was mentioned there: Jeremiah Hirsch, born March 16, 1910. So he had just become 33. I called out his name, and from the abyss of silence just one word came back: "*Hinneni,*" which means, as I know now, "here I am." This was his answer, from the book of *Genesis*, out of the depths. I helped him pack his backbag; and he comforted me, he, Jeremiah, my friend, my brother. In the early morning I did my usual job, bring the procession to the train. He was there among many other people, parents and children, he with his Lea and his children, a boy and a girl about seven years of age. He walked with difficulty. He limped and his backbag was heavy. There were perhaps more books in it than usual, although he held in his hand the small black book which I had seen so often with him, for a backbag could easily get lost, could it not? On the platform he stumbled, and because of this, he dropped the small book. He bent down with the greatest difficulty (ah, that back bag!) to pick it up, but Cohn beat him to it. Cohn kicked it away and pulled him roughly to the train. During a short discussion, which I could not understand, Cohn gave him a bloody nose, while Schaufinger watched, laughing.

Then it happened faster than I can tell it. I flew towards Cohn and hit him on his face with full force. I turned, picked up the small book, and gave it back to the rebbe. As he stood near the entrance to the cattle car, I still feel how he put his hands on my head and murmured some words. I could not understand them then, but now I know what they mean. Only then did I heard the loud laugh of Schaufinger. Slapping his thighs, he exclaimed, "Nah, Cohn, after all you are also nothing else but a little Yid!"[12] Cohn, whiter than a ghost, was beside himself with fury and shouted a few words to a couple of Disposition Service men[13] who chased me with kicks and beatings to this building, the punishment barracks.

In this barracks I again met Dé.[14] She sat there, staring ahead. Finally she stood up, came over to me, and stroked my hair.

"Come on, Dé, say something, please!

She smiled. "Next week, when we sit in the train, I have to digest so many things and there are so many questions. Why did you beat up Cohn and not Schaufinger? No, don't try to explain it. You can do that when we are in the train. In the train to Sobibor. Anyway, from now on I give you back your own first name: Jacob."

Notes:

1 After I had translated this story, the J. M. Meulenhoff Publishing Company informed me in 1998 that it had sold the exclusive English translation rights to The Harvill Press in London, England. The Harvill Press approved use of my translation and informed me that their book, a translation of Presser's story by Barrows Mussey, is now out of print. Primo Levi, who introduced the English translation of the novella, wrote, "This brief work is one of the few that gives literary voice to Western European [*Sephardim*] Judaism in a fitting manner."

2 Westerbork was a large collection/transit camp in the northeastern Neth-

erlands. From mid-1942 through 1944 more than 100,000 Jews were transported to Westerbork. From there they were transported east to the extermination camps.

3 Georg was a pupil of the author Henriques, a Portuguese Jew and history teacher at an Amsterdam high school. Georg was the son of Cohn, another Jewish collaborator who became the boss of Henriques in the Westerbork camp. Georg himself became a black marketeer making easily lots of money as long as he was free, under the protection of his father.

4 Every concentration camp had its own internal authority structure, which the Nazis called its *self-government*. Each barracks had its own responsible head (*Dienstleiter*) and these heads were accountable to the Chief of Staff and his assistant (also prisoners). They in turn were accountable to the SS Commander, a Nazi. In this story the Commander is Kurt Schaufinger, the Chief of Staff is Cohn, and his assistant, the author of the story, is Jacob Henriques. As long as Cohn and Henriques were able to maintain their position, they were free from the threat of deportation.

5 The Dutch government with Queen Wilhelmina escaped to London in 1940 when Germany attacked the Netherlands.

6 This council was instituted in 1567 by Duke Alba, who took over the government of the Low Countries from Margaretha, the half-sister of Philip II, King of Spain. The official name of this Council was Council of Unrest, but the people soon called it the Council of Blood because of its cruel, bloody decisions.

7 The first name of Cohn.

8 His dog.

9 Those who are going to die greet him.

10 Well-known, endearing title for a rabbi, similar to "our reverend."

11 Sobibor, in east-central Poland, was one of the six killing centers that the Nazis established in occupied Poland.

12 Abusive term for a Jew.

13 Policemen who served in the Ordnung Dienst.

14 Dé was a courier girl of the resistance movement and had been arrested in the train near Amersfoort [about 50 kilometers (30 miles) east of Amsterdam].

chapter twenty
IN MEMORIAM

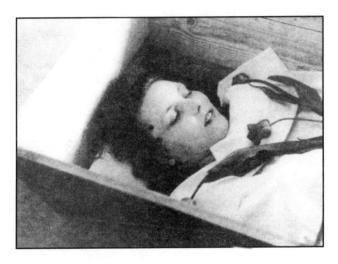

This book would not be complete without an "in memoriam" for those who did not survive.

This picture comes from a booklet, long out of print, titled *Nazihel* (*Nazi Hell*).[1] The booklet consists of documents collected and commented on by the Dutch war-photographer Willem van de Pol.

The picture caption translated is:

> *Triumphant in Death. This is a well-known underground hero. Married for only fourteen days, she and her husband were shot to death by Nazi brutes on the eve of the liberation of Deventer, a city in the Eastern part of the Netherlands.*

Where was God that terrible evening? Cynics might say, "God was not there or God is dead." I don't believe this to be true. I believe that in His inscrutable wisdom God wrote a page with two sides. On one side He wrote "The Hell of sin." But on the other side He wrote "The heaven of the righteous freedom-fighter." And God gave this book to us to read and to remember.

Look at the picture. Here she is, young and beautiful, a flower broken in the bud. What more can be said about her? I don't know her name, her family, her hopes, her dreams. Shall we say, "She did not make it—too bad"?

No, I refuse to end this book in such resignation. Life's value cannot be expressed in a measure of quantity. What counts is quality. This woman brought messages from one commander of the underground to the other, often hiding them on her body under her clothes. She served. She worked for freedom.

Yes, dear heroine freedom-lover, we will remember you and all the others who lost or gave their lives. We live because you died. We will remember you and honor you.

Notes

1 The booklet was published by Van Holkema & Warendorf and distributed by Unieboek Publishing, Houten, The Netherlands.

CONTRIBUTORS

CLARA ASSCHER-PINKHOF
Chapter 6

EVA BROSS
Chapter 7

RITA HERZBERG
LISTER
Chapter 11

TOM FALUDI
Chapter 8

JERZY TADEUSZ
PINDERA

Chapters 15 & 16

REMKES KOOISTRA
Chapter 17